AF564524

The Emergence of Peasant Politics in Haryana, 1920-46

The Emergence of Peasant Politics in Haryana, 1920-46

AJAYVIR SINGH

LG PUBLISHERS DISTRIBUTORS

First Published, 2015

ISBN 978-93-83723-11-9

Published by
LG PUBLISHERS DISTRIBUTORS
49, Gali No. 14, Pratap Nagar
Mayur Vihar Phase I, Delhi 110 091
Tel : 011 2279 5641 email: lgpdist@gmail.com

Printed at
D.K. Fine Art Press (P) Ltd., Delhi

for
My Parents

Contents

List of Tables

Acknowledgements

I would like to express my thanks to all who contributed in the preparation of this book. My special thanks are due to Professor Mridula Mukherjee and Professor Aditya Mukherjee for their advice and guidance. I express my gratitude to Professor Dilbag Singh for his valuable suggestions and encouragements. I owe a special debt to Professor Syed Inayat Ali Zaidi and Professor Sunita Zaidi for their parental love and support. I am also grateful to Professor K.C. Yadav who generously gave suggestions for this book.

I am also thankful to the staff of the Nehru Memorial Museum and Library, National Archives of India, Indian Council of Historical Research, Jawaharlal Nehru University Library, Haryana Academy of History and Culture and Haryana State Archives for their constant help during the completion of this work.

I would like to thank Amardeep, Narender Yadav, Rajesh Kumar, Naushad Ali. Jagdish Prashad, Ajay Jacob Thomas and Mahender Singh for their help by which it became easy for me to complete this book. Lastly, I would also like to thank my family for providing me their support when ever I needed.

Ajayvir Singh

Abbreviations

BEIP	–	Board of Economic Inquiry, Punjab
FR	–	Fortnightly Report
HAHC	–	Haryana Academy of History and Culture
HSA	–	Haryana State Archives
ICHR	–	Indian Council of Historical Research
INA	–	Indian National Army
JNU	–	Jawaharlal Nehru University
NAI	–	National Archives of India
NMML	–	Nehru Memorial Museum and Library
PLAD	–	Punjab Legislative Assembly Debates
PLCD	–	Punjab Legislative Council Debates

Introduction

Haryana (or the south-east region of colonial Punjab) from 1920 to 1946 was in a transition phase. During this period many divergent political trends emerged. The Indian National Movement was approaching the peasantry in the countryside to acquire a mass base. The 1919 Government of India Act introduced separate electorates for urban and rural areas. The rural masses, mostly peasants, began to participate in political activities by joining political organizations and parties. They actively started to participate in rallies and demonstrations. The rural and agrarian issues dominated the politics of this region for more than two decades. In this period due to high land revenue rates and poor agrarian conditions, rural poverty, moneylending and agricultural indebtedness had become important characteristics of the agrarian economy.

During the freedom struggle the mobilization of the peasantry was started by Mahatma Gandhi. He led the peasant struggle against the indigo planters in Champaran and land revenue system in Kaira in Gujarat. Mahatma Gandhi raised the peasants' issues at the national level.

The peasant politics of Haryana can be studied at three levels—at the national level, at the provincial level and at the regional level. There has been very little specialized historical work on this area because, for the most part, it has been studied as a part of a larger province, i.e. the colonial Punjab or undivided Punjab before independence. The historians of modern India have not discussed the peasantry of this region at length.

This book has been divided into four chapters excluding the introduction and conclusion. The first chapter examines the socio-economic condition of the peasants. It describes the castes and tribes of the peasantry. It answers many questions like what were the peasants' grievances? Why were the peasants of Haryana backward? The issues of rural poverty, land revenue and indebtedness are analysed in this chapter. The second chapter deals with the politicization process of peasants in the region of Haryana. It also analyses the elections held in Haryana from 1920 to 1946.

The third chapter deals with political participation of peasants in the nationalist movement particularly in the Non-Cooperation Movement, Civil Disobedience Movement and the Quit India Movement. It studies the ideology and political consciousness of peasantry. The fourth and last chapter critically examines the various legislative measures taken by the Punjab provincial government to empower the peasantry. What stand did the political parties take on these legislations? How did the peasants respond to these legislations? This chapter answers these questions.

1

Peasants' Society and Economy

I. PEASANTS' SOCIETY

Haryana was the south-east region of colonial Punjab or undivided Punjab before the partition of India. It comprises five districts—Ambala, Karnal, Gurgaon, Rohtak and Hissar. The social composition of peasants in these districts was as follows:

In Ambala the Jats, Rajputs, Gujars and Arains were the chief peasant castes. The Arains villages occupied a large area in Ropar tehsil. Chauhan Rajputs held a considerable area in the Ambala tehsil. Jats occupied a more or less compact area in many parts of the district and there were Sainis scattered throughout, Brahmans and Sayads held smaller groups of territory.[1]

Karnal district was formed out of the old Sikh states of Thanesar, Ladwa and Kaithal. This district represented the territory of Karnal and Panipat tehsils. Rajputs, Afghans, Brahmans known as 'Taga' and Jats were the peasants in this district.[2]

Gurgaon district occupied the extreme south-east corner of the province. It was distinguished by having a large number of villages of a particular tribe called 'Meo' and there were also Ahirs and Jats settled in some numbers.[3]

1. B.H. Baden–Powell, *The Land System of British India,* reprint, London, 1972, p. 682.
2. Ibid., p. 684.
3. Ibid., p. 687.

Rohtak district had a large preponderance of Jats, who held the majority of estates. There were also villages of other peasant castes such as Rajputs, Brahmans, Afghans, Rangars, Gujars and Biluch.[4]

In Hissar district Jats, Rajputs, Brahmans, Pathans, Bishnois and Saiyeds were peasants. Bhiwani tahsil was occupied by Jats and Rajputs. Hansi tehsil was almost occupied by Jats. In Hissar tehsil Jats and Rajputs were the main peasant castes. Most part of Fatehabad tehsil was held by Jats. Sirsa tehsil contained several Jat villages.[5]

Thus we see that in these districts of Haryana the main peasant castes were Jats, Rajputs, Ahirs, Gujars, Sainis, Sayeds, Afghans, Rangars, etc. A few Brahmans were agriculturists. These peasant castes were also called agriculturist tribes. The agricultural tribes notified under the Land Alienation Act (XIII of 1900) were Ahirs, Bilochs, Gujars, Jats, Malis, Moghals, Pathans, Rajputs, Rors, Saiyeds and Gaur Brahmans (excluding Bohras).[6]

Of the non-agricultural tribes, the Chamars were the most important. They gave a great deal of assistance, either in return for a share of the crop, or as day-labourers, in the actual processes of agriculture. They were usually very poor, and were in danger of starvation when the crop failed. The Dhanaks and Chuhras, who were not often found together, were the village scavengers. The Dhanaks were also weavers. Khatiks or tanners were found in a few villages. The Kumhars (potters), Chhipis (tailors and dye–stampers), Jhinwars (water–carriers and molasses–cooks), Telis (oilmen), carpenters (who were usually Khatis and sometimes Barhis) and Lohars (blacksmiths) were the other important menial and non-agriculturist tribes.[7]

---

4. Ibid.
5. *Gazetteer of Hissar District, 1892*, p. 118.
6. *Gazetteer of Rohtak District, 1910*, p. 78.
7. Ibid., pp. 78-79.

The general characteristics of the peasants according to their castes are as follows—the Jat was "lord of the land" and when asked who he is, replies "zamindar" before he says "Jat". They are very clannish and cherish the memories of ancient feuds. They are shrewd and love a joke when they master it.[8] Rohtak Jats are a powerful, war like, fine and sturdy race of cultivators.[9] According to a handbook, "A Jat of Rohtak is far from turbulent but is independent and self-willed. He is usually content to cultivate his field in quietness if people will let him do so. No one could be associated with Jats for anytime without conceiving both respect and liking for them."[10] The Jat was considered as a typical yeoman, the finest farmer in Northern India. His knowledge of crops and cattle was unrivalled, and his industry was unceasing. Every member of the family, from the old crone down to tiny children, shared in the field-work.[11] Rohtak peasants were manly without false pride, independent without insolence, good-natured, light-hearted and industrious."[12]

The Rors ranked with the Jats whom they closely resemble. The Ahirs were also agriculturists. Like the Jats they practised widow marriage.[13] The Ahirs of Gurgaon and adjacent districts differed marginally if at all from his Jat neighbour, and was equally brave, industrious and orderly. The Hindu Gujar on the other hand though closely resembling the Ahir and Jat in manners and customs was an indifferent cultivator and much preferred the care of cattle to the toil of agricultural labour.[14] The Jats occupied the social

---

8. Ibid., pp. 76-77.
9. G.F. Macmunn, *Armies of India,* London, 1911, pp. 160-161.
10. A.H. Bingley, *Handbook for the Indian Army: Jats, Gujars and Ahirs,* New Delhi 1941, p. 52.
11. W. Crooke, *Races of Northern India,* Delhi, 1973, p. 92.
12. *Settlement Report of Rohtak District, 1880,* p. 72.
13. *Gazetteer of Rohtak District, 1910,* pp. 76-77.
14. A.H. Bingley, *Handbook for the Indian Army: Jats, Gujars and Ahirs,* New Delhi, 1941, p. 52 .

position shared by Ahirs and Gujars, all three ate and smoked together.[15]

The Brahmans were purohits as well as cultivators.[16] Unlike many other parts of India, in Haryana the Brahmans were also agriculturists. War pestilence and famine, it is said, often compelled the younger members of these communities to seek employment in the military.[17]

The Muslim Rajputs are described as good soldiers and indifferent cultivators. They generally preferred to let their lands rather than till them in person.[18]

Rural society was divided into religions and each religion by caste, for example: Hindu, Muslim, Sikh, Jain, Christian, Buddhist and others and the castes like agriculturist castes (Jat, Rajput, Ahir, Gujar, Saini, Mali, Meo, etc.), the religious castes (Brahman, Shekh, Saiyed), the mercantile castes (Arora, Bania, Khatri), the artisan castes (Machhi, Kumhar, Nai, Sunar, Lohar, etc.), the menial and outcaste (Chamar, Chuhra and Dhanak), etc.[19]

In Haryana "caste is a social far more than a religious institution".[20] Occupation was the primary basis of caste. "The whole basis of diversity of caste is diversity of occupation. The old division into Brahman, Kshatriya, Vaisya, Sudra and the Mlechchha or outcaste who is below the Sudra, is but a division into the priest, the warrior, the husbandman, the artisan, and the menial."[21] The "caste" is therefore based on distinctions of occupation rather than concepts of higher or lower 'types' and 'races'.

---

15. Ibid., also W. Crook, *Races of Northern India*, Delhi, 1973, p. 115.
16. *Gazetteer of Rohtak District*, 1910, pp. 76-77.
17. A.H. Bingley, *Caste Handbooks for the Indian Army, Brahmans,* Simla, 1897, p. 8.
18. *Gazetteers of Rohtak District, 1910*, pp. 76-77.
19. *Census of Punjab, 1881, Report,* p. 107.
20. Denzil Ibbetson, *Panjab Castes,* 1916, p. 2.
21. Ibid., p. 3.

The caste in the late 19th and early 20th century was based on occupation and within an occupation on political prominence and social standing. Social standing was dependent on caste and caste on social standing, for the two depend each on the other in different senses. The rise in the social scale was followed by a rise in caste while the fall in the grades of caste surely accompanied by loss of social standing.[22]

'Caste' differentials were therefore based on distinctions of occupation, individual achievement and political resources. In Haryana occupation was divided on the basis of caste. Every caste had its own occupation. For example, the people who were engaged in agriculture were categorized as the agriculturist caste or tribe. The occupation of agriculturists or peasants in the Punjab was husbandry and cattle farming. They were also the owners of the land.[23] But in Haryana mostly peasants had small plots of land and they cultivated their land by family labour or hired labour. These peasants were called the agriculturist tribe.

There were also some instances of mutability of caste. The Brahmans were generally husbandmen in Haryana. And when a Brahman dropped in sacerdotal character, he ceased to receive food or alms as offerings acceptable to gods, and became a cultivator, he also ceased to be a Brahman, and had to employ other Brahmans as priests. For example, Brahmans who had "abandoned" (tag dena) their priestly character became Tagas.[24] The people of the 'Chauhan' tribe in the Karnal region whose fathers were 'born Rajput', but who had taken to weaving and had become Shekhs.[25] In Sirsa there were instances of clans who were a few generations ago accounted Jats but later classed as Rajputs because

22. Ibid., p. 6.
23. Ibid., p. 5.
24. Ibid., p. 6.
25. Ibid., p. 8.

during the time they practised greater exclusiveness in matrimonial matters, and had abandoned widow marriage. The Chauhans of Delhi were no longer recognized as Rajputs since they had begun to marry their widows. There were also traditions of the Punjab that those Rajputs who married below them, ceased to seclude their women, or began to practise widow marriage got status of the Jats and Gujars.[26] And the distinction between the Jats and Rajputs, both sprung from a common Indo-Aryan stock (race), was marked by the fact that the former practise and the latter abstain from widow marriage.[27] In this way, every caste had their own occupation and customs and those who changed their occupation and customs also changed their caste.

The Rajputs and the Jats in Haryana were considered as branches of the same race. The Rajputs represented those members of the groups who maintained the purity of the blood and a high standard of orthodox Hindu life. The Jats failing to satisfy these requirements had sunk to a lower level by devoting themselves to farming, by sanctioning widow re-marriage and allowing their women to work in the fields.[28]

Among the artisan and menial tribes the process was more common. For example, one Chamar who took to weaving instead of tanning became a Chamar-Julaha, another did the same and became a Rangreta or a Bunia, and a Chuhra refused to touch night soil and became a Musalli or Kutana. Within castes as well the same process was observable. The Chander Chamar did not eat or marry a Jatia Chamar because the latter worked with the hides of impure animals. One section of the Kumhars would hold no communion with another because the latter burnt garbage as fuel, a third section had taken to agriculture and looked

---

26. Ibid., pp. 7-8.
27. H.H. Risley, *The People of India,* Calcutta and Simla, 1915, pp. 93-94.
28. W. Crooke, *Races of Northern India,* Delhi, 1973, p. 92.

down on both.[29] In this way, diversities existed not only in different castes but were also found within the same caste.

In Haryana conversion from Hinduism to Islam had no effect on the caste of the convert. The Muslim Rajput, Gujar or Jat was for all social, tribal, political and administrative purposes exactly as much a Rajput, Gujar or Jat as his Hindu brother. His social customs are unaltered, his tribal restrictions are unreleased, his rules of marriage and inheritance unchanged.[30]

The Haryanavi society was also divided into tribes. And the tribal communities held together by the tie of common descent, each tribe being self-contained and self-sufficient and bound by strict rules of marriage and inheritance. According to him all these strengthened and preserved the unity of the tribe. The 'tribe' was the universal fact of rural life in Haryana, not 'caste'. About tribal divisions among the landowning castes, within the caste the first great division of the landowning classes was into tribes and the tribe was far more permanent and indestructible than the caste.[31]

About social intercourse between castes, no superior tribe would eat or drink from the hands or vessels of an inferior one, or smoke its pipes. Jats, Gujars, Rors, Rahbaris and Ahirs ate and drank in common without any scruples. Brahmans and Rajputs would not eat from any one below a Jat, Gujar, or Ror, while these three tribes themselves did not as a rule eat or drink with any of the menial castes which were considered absolutely impure owing to their occupation and habits, and their mere touch defiled food. The menial castes were leather-makers, washermen, barbers, blacksmiths, dyers, sweepers etc. The potter was also looked upon as of doubtful purity. The pipes of a village, being often left about in the common rooms and fields, were generally

29. Denzil Ibbetson, op.cit., p. 8.
30. Ibid., pp. 13-14.
31. Ibid., p. 16.

distinguished by a piece of something tied around the stem-blue rag for Muslim, red for Hindu, leather for a Chamar, string for a sweeper and so forth, so that a friend wishing for a smoke might not defile himself by mistake.[32] In this way caste segregation was prevalent in the society. Upper castes always tried to distinguish themselves from the lower castes. But in rural society all castes worked and lived together and played an important role in the agrarian economy. However, every caste had its own occupation.

Caste in itself was rigid amongst the higher castes, but malleable amongst the lower. The British pigeon-holed everyone by castes and deplored the caste system and its effect on social and economic problems.[33]

When a person of low caste wished to return himself as belonging to a high caste to which he obviously did not belong, for example, a 'Teli' wished to return himself as a 'Moghal' he should be shown as belonging to the caste or tribe to which he was generally supposed to belong. Again, if a 'Jat or Sunar' wished to be entered as 'Rajput' he should not be entered as a Rajput if the people did not call him a Rajput. And the members of the Arya Samaj, those said that they had abandoned caste or did not wish to had any caste recorded, may be entered as Arya by caste.[34]

The caste or tribe of an unmarried girl would be the same as that of her father. In respect of a married woman the entry should be as stated by her husband. No enquiry should be made as to the caste or tribe of a woman before her marriage. Her caste or tribe should be checked and the answer accepted without question. Among Hindus the caste of a woman would be that of her husband but among Muslims the husband in some cases, liked to have one of his wives put down as Pathani, the other as Jatti and the third as a

32. Denzil Ibbetson, op.cit., p. 25.
33. *Census of Punjab. 1921, Report*, p. 345.
34. Ibid., p. 341.

Bilochni.[35]

The peasants were divided further into gentes or 'gots'. The tribe as a whole was strictly endogamous. But every tribe was divided into gentes and these gentes were strictly exogamous. The tribes from a common ancestor or common descent could not intermarry.[36]

Amongst Hindus the commonest rule of exogamy was what might be called the four-got rule.

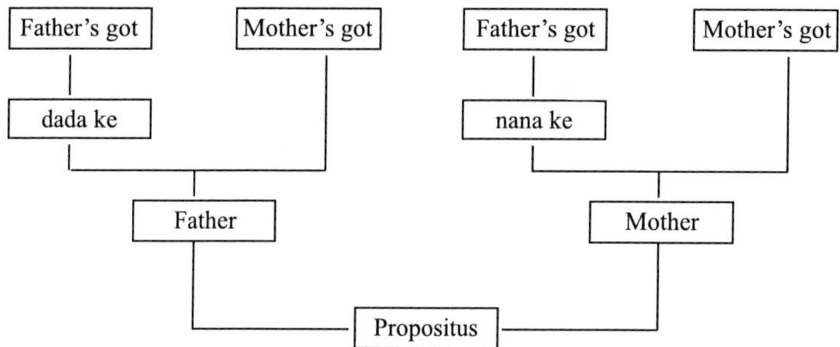

In the Ambala district it was stated that the four-got rule was observed by the Chuhra, Banjara, Julaha, Ramdasia Chamar and Kalal castes, while the Agarwal Banias, Sikh Jats and Hindu Malis were content to avoid one, i.e. the father's got alone, and the Hindu Lohar avoided only three. The Jats as a whole married outside the tribe, which thus represented the got and avoided the usual four 'gots' in marriage. In Haryana inter-marriage between tribes of common descent was usually avoided.[37]

II. PEASANTS' ECONOMY

Due to agricultural backwardness and high land revenue rates, rural poverty and indebtedness had become main features of the agrarian economy. These agrarian issues and

35. Ibid., p. 342.
36. *Settlement Report of the Karnal Disrict, 1883*, p. 77.
37. *Census of Punjab, 1901, Report*, pp. 326, 332.

grievances culminated in rural unrest and social conflict.

Peasants' Structure of Landholding

Haryana or the south-east region of colonial Punjab was a region of petty peasant proprietors. But their proprietary rights existed only till they paid the land revenue. The state was supreme landlord and retained important rights of resumption for failure to pay the land revenue or for refusal to accept the new demand at settlement. The settlement was a bilateral contract between the state and the village owners. The village owners had the right to appeal against the demand and to reject it and their rights in land. Their hard legal option to accept the demand or abandon the village was in practice.[38]

Therefore the proprietary rights of the peasant existed only till he paid the land revenue. If he was not in a position to pay the land revenue, he lost his proprietary rights and even had to abandon the village.

Table 1.1: Percentage of Holdings Owned in Various Size Categories: British Southeast Punjab: District-wise Figures (1920s)

Holding Size Category	*Hissar*	*Rohtak*	*Gurgaon*	*Karnal*	*Ambala*
Under 1 acre	6.5	7.1	10.3	11.4	21.7
1-5 acres	28.7	38.8	45.5	42.7	45.0
5-10 acres	21.9	25.2	22.2	23.6	17.6
10-15 acres	13.2	11.5	9.8	10.3	6.9
15-20 acres	8.0	7.6	4.4	4.9	3.0
20-25 acres	5.4	3.8	2.5	2.2	1.9
25-30 acres	10.3	4.7	3.6	3.9	1.7
Over 50 acres	6.1	1.3	1.5	1.6	1.9

Source: Mridula Mukherjee, *Colonializing Agriculture: The Myth of Punjab Exceptionalism,* New Delhi, 2005, pp. 108-109.

38. H. Calvert, *The Wealth and Welfare of the Punjab,* Lahore, 1936, pp. 169-170.

The district-wise figures show that the great majority of Haryana peasants owned very small plots of land of less than five acres.

The big peasants who had over fifty acres of land were very few in Haryana district, i.e. less than two per cent, except Hissar where they were around six per cent. In this way, Haryana was primarily a land of small peasant proprietors who cultivated their land by family labour supplemented by hired labour as needed.

Agricultural Backwardness

Agriculture was the main occupation of the rural people in Haryana. In this region agriculture had developed much less due to lack of rainfall and artificial means of irrigation compared to canal colonies in the western part and the central districts of colonial Punjab.[39]

In Haryana most of the people who lived in villages were dependent on agriculture and agriculture was dependent on rainfall because of lack of irrigation facilities in this region. This region was far away from the perennial rivers and the river Jamuna flowed along the eastern boundary of the state. The non-perennial river Ghaggar which passed through the northern parts caused considerable yearly damage to the agriculture in this area. In this region rainfall was low and erratic and in the months of July to September often there were floods. The soil was sandy and light in texture and the level of sub-soil water was very deep, about twenty-five to one hundred and fifty feet.[40]

---

39. Himadri Banerjee, 'Changes in Agrarian Society in the Late Nineteenth Century' in *Five Punjabi Centuries: Polity, Economy, Society and Culture, C. 1500-1900,* edited by Indu Banga, New Delhi, 1997, p. 333.
40. Prem Chowdhry, 'The Advantages of Backwardness: Colonial Policy and Agriculture in Haryana, in *The Economic and Social History Review*, 23, 3 (1986), New Delhi, p. 264.

Agriculture in this region depended on extensive irrigation and this facility was absent here. Without irrigation this region continued to remain agriculturally backward than other parts of British colonial Punjab.[41]

The dry and hot climate and the dry sandy soil were the physical features of Haryana. Though rainfall was scanty, only a few showers were enough in the monsoon to produce a plentiful crop of excellent grasses both in the cultivated field and on the sandy hillock which were a marked feature of more arid tracts. In dry seasons the scarcity of fodder forced the animals to roam and it resulted in exercise which was better for the cattle.[42]

Therefore this region seemed eminently suitable for cattle, and the British had realized that "Haryana produced cattle greatly in excess of its own requirements."[43] It had a near monopoly of cattle sales in British Punjab. Haryana contributed ninety-nine per cent of the sale of cattle in British Punjab in 1939 and over half the total number of cattle traded in all India.[44]

However, animal husbandry could not remain unaffected in the chronically drought-prone region, which suffered from famines and fodder scarcity.[45] In the fodder scarcity years, the prices of fodder rose sharply, e.g. in 1931 by nearly seventy per cent.[46] Peasants had to pay very high prices for fodder due to which the prices of cattle fell dramatically, thereby reducing the owner's wealth.

---

41. Ibid., pp. 264-265.
42. H.K. Trevaskis, *An Economic History of Punjab (1890-1925)*, Vol. II, First Published, Lahore 1931, second edition, New Delhi, 1989, p. 363.
43. A.M. Stowe, *Cattle and Dairying in the Punjab,* Lahore, 1910, p. 67, cited in Prem Chowdhry, *op.cit,* p. 265.
44. Ibid.
45. Ibid., p. 269.
46. M.L. Darling, *Wisdom and Waste in the Punjab Village,* Reprint, Delhi, 1977, see preface.

Because of uncertainty in agriculture conditions and frequent famines leading to heavy cattle mortality, animal husbandry did not become a highly paying proposition for the peasants.[47]

The crop pattern in Haryana was also different from other parts of British Punjab. This region focused on low value food-cum-fodder crops, with increasing acreage under fodder cultivation and an attempt to curb the limited efforts made at substitution of fodder crops by other crops without irrigation. In this region peasants grew only drought resisting crops and hardy varieties e.g. in the Rabi season, they grew gram, barley, wheat and sarson, and in Kharif they grew 'juar', 'bajra' 'guara' and 'moth'. Therefore, due to lack of irrigation facilities peasants had to grow crops which needed less water.

There was a great demand for fodder for animals and food for themselves but due to lack of irrigation facilities, and also the fact that the colonial government having already created for exports a massive wheat basket elsewhere in the Punjab, it hardly gave wheat in Haryana any incentive. The government was only concerned with the cultivation of other crops in this region.[48] Therefore, in this region the peasants grew only drought-resistant crops.

The crops of rice and sugarcane both needed a great deal of water, which was not available and also a heavy initial investment. Therefore rice featured nowhere in the region but sugarcane because of the heavy local demand for 'gur' (raw sugar) and refined sugar continued to be produced on a limited scale. The small irrigated parts of Rohtak and Karnal districts came to represent the sugar-growing tracts under the British.[49] The other reason may be that compared to rice, sugarcane needed less water. Therefore peasants

47. Prem Chowdhry, op. cit., p. 272.
48. Ibid., p. 276.
49. Ibid.

grew the sugarcane in this region.

But in most parts of Haryana, like other parts of India, agriculture depended largely on the rains and failure of rain was a common phenomenon in this region. Therefore, economic conditions of the peasants were always precarious.[50]

Land Revenue

The British adopted a variety of systems for collection of land revenue—the zamindari system, the Ryotwari system, Mahalwari system. In the Punjab, a village-based system—a modified version of the Mahalwari system was introduced.

After a long debate between British officials, they appointed 'settlement officers' to decide the amount of land revenue. Cash assessments were fixed for terms of twenty or thirty years after which reassessment was made. A valuable register of land titles was drawn up for all agricultural land throughout the province and steps were gradually taken to keep it up-to-date.[51]

The first settlements of the region (Delhi, Gurgaon and Karnal districts) were made under the North-Western Province government. They expired in or before 1872, and revisions were then carried out. Rohtak was settled in 1873-9. Hissar was settled in 1863 for twenty years. The Sirsa re-settlement was finished in 1882 and this district had been abolished and divided between Hissar and Firozpur. The first Ambala settlements had been undertaken piecemeal as the district was not completely formed at one date. The Thanesar portion was settled in 1869. Finally the settlements were so sanctioned that the period of the several portions

50. Himadri Banerjee, *Agrarian Society of the Punjab (1849-1901)*, New Delhi, 1982, p. 105.
51. H.K. Trevaskis, *An Economic History of Punjab (1890-1925)*, Vol. II, First Published, Lahore,1931, second edition, New Delhi, 1989, p. 150.

should expire together in 1880. The re-settlement was then completed.[52]

After these settlements the cultivator knew how much rent he had to pay, and he was secured against further exactions, authorized or unauthorized. The prevalence of the peasant proprietor became the main feature of the agricultural economy of the province.[53] The peasant could sell, mortgage, and alienate his land. This was to the advantage of the government because it could auction his land in case he could not pay the land revenue.

There were many problems with the British land revenue system. The land revenue had increased owing to extension of cultivation and the increase in prices of produce, but the potential profits had been swallowed up by the rising cost of cultivation. The cost of bullocks, ploughs, manure, etc. had increased much more than prices of agricultural produce. Self-cultivating peasants did not benefit from this. Only landlords benefited who gave their land on batai or share-cropping and received half the gross produce in the form of rent, but paid very little towards the cost of cultivation.[54]

The system of land revenue assessment concerned itself only with the value of the produce and ignored the cost of cultivation. The calculations made no allowance for wages of tenants or family labour expended on farms or for profits of cultivation. And the yield estimates were too high because they were based on holdings operating under ideal conditions. The land revenue assessments were made on the basis of the average price of the whole year, whereas the small peasants, who were the vast majority of revenue

52. B.H. Baden–Powell, *The Land Systems of British India*, London, 1972, see footnotes, p. 543.
53. H.K. Trevaskis, op. cit., p. 150.
54. Mridula Mukherjee, 'Some Aspects of Agrarian Structure of Punjab, 1925-47' in *Economic and Political Weekly*, Vol. XV, No. 26, June 1980, p. A-47.

payers, sold their produce soon after the harvest when prices were at their lowest.[55]

In other words, land assessment was based on the value of the produce and it ignored the cost of cultivation. The land revenue assessment was based on the average prices of the whole year. Small peasants had to sell their produce at the lowest rates to pay the revenue. Therefore they did not benefit from the high prices.

The smaller peasants also had to bear the rigidity of land revenue collection. His petty income ruled out any possibility of building up reserves for lean years and the land revenue was the first charge on his production even in the bad years. Therefore indebtedness was often the only way to meet his consumption requirements.[56] In this way small peasants had to borrow money from the moneylenders to pay the land revenue and for their daily consumption in the year of scarcity.

To counter the growing criticism of rigidity of the existing system a new system of fluctuating assessment called the sliding-scale system was introduced in 1935. By this system they fixed a corresponding set of maximum revenue rates based on the prices of the last twenty years. When prices remained below these "commutation prices", revenue rates would be correspondingly reduced, but if the actual prices exceeded commutation prices, the revenue rate would not go beyond the maximum rates. The Punjab Land Revenue Committee in its reports in 1938 specifically recommended that the sliding-scale system should not be extended to small-holding districts because this system was linked only to prices of agriculture produce and did not take into account the variations in the cost of cultivation.[57]

---

55. Ibid., p. A-49.
56. Mridula Mukherjee, *Colonializing Agriculture: The Myth of Punjab Exceptionalism*, New Delhi, 2005, p. 19.
57. Ibid., p. 21.

Thus, a large proportion of the peasants could not benefit from agriculture because of the rise in costs of cultivation and from animal husbandry because of rise in the prices of fodder and animal foods.

Indebtedness

In the second half of the 19th century the growing indebtedness of the peasants and the transfer of landed property by mortgage and sale to urban moneylenders became the common phenomenon of the agrarian economy not only in Haryana but in all of British Punjab. There was serious agrarian unrest due to loss of land by the peasantry. The government adopted various measures to meet this political threat, but by far the most drastic was the enactment in 1900 of the Punjab Alienation of Land Act which prohibited the transfer of land from the agriculturalist tribes to non-agriculturalist in the Punjab.[58] After this Act a class of agriculturalist moneylenders emerged who furnished capital to their fellow cultivators. Land transfer was not stopped or even slackened by the alienation restrictions. Only the direction of the flow of land was altered.[59] Therefore the number of agriculturist moneylenders increased after this Act. Indebtedness and the transfer of land from peasants to moneylenders continued. The peasants' condition did not improve.

The growing commercialization, the introduction of a fixed inelastic revenue demand, the occurrence of famines and the fragmentation of holdings created a market which led indirectly to universal indebtedness among the landholders of the Punjab.[60] In this way indebtedness among

58. Norman G. Barrier, 'The Formulation and Enactment of the Punjab Alienation of Land Bill', in *The Punjab Past and Present*, Vol. XIII-I, April 1979, S. No. 25, Punjabi University, Patiala, p. 193.
59. Ibid., p. 214.
60. Himadri Banerjee, 'Changes in Agrarian Society in the Late

the peasants had become the main feature of the agrarian economy in the Punjab. Almost every section of the peasantry was in debt whether small or big.

An official estimate of 1899-1900 showed that sale of land had increased by nearly 431 per cent since 1865, while the number of mortgages increased by about 200 per cent between 1875 and 1900. In a number of districts, the bulk of these transfers went in favour of the professional non-agriculturist moneylenders among the Banias, Khatris and Aroras.[61] The moneylenders reaped a huge profit by mixing inferior grains with wheat and by raising the prices.[62]

The moneylenders were also involved in various malpractices. They charged highest rates of interest. Debt was misrepresented in the ledger by entering inferior grains as if they were wheat. Accounts were often kept in such 'a loose and unintelligible' way that the interest could not be separated from the principal. These accounts were also maintained in the Landa script which the sahukars alone could understand. Another interesting aspect of this credit transaction was its tendency to accumulate without limit. [63]

The moneylenders attempted to exact a higher rate of rent from the peasant mortgagors and the process of transfer of land to sahukars deeply affected the rural economy of the province.[64] By 1929 the total debt in the Punjab province was over 330 crores, if the debt was evenly distributed among the population, each person would owe more than one year's income to the moneylender. The Punjab Banking Enquiry Commission found that moneylending to the agriculturists

---

Nineteenth Century, in *Five Punjabi Centuries: Polity, Economy, Society and Culture, C. 1500-1900,* edited by Indu Banga, New Delhi, 1997, p. 337.

61. Ibid.
62. Himadri Banerjee, *Agrarian Society of the Punjab (1849-1901),* New Delhi, 1982, p. 105.
63. Ibid., p. 117.
64. Ibid., p. 122.

had become the Punjab's largest industry.[65] In this way, the agrarian economy was affected by the indebtedness and transfer of land to the moneylenders. Moneylending in Haryana was the important institution during the colonial period.

In the three districts of Haryana—Karnal, Rohtak and Gurgaon—non-agriculturist moneylenders had a stronghold and they contributed 60 per cent or more of those taxed.[66] But in Rohtak village, the number of agriculturist moneylenders was double that of all other classes of moneylenders put together.[67] Although the number of agriculturist moneylenders was more than non-agriculturist moneylenders, yet non-agriculturist moneylenders still had a hold over the moneylending business because they had a larger share in this business. A survey of Gijhi village in Rohtak district in 1925 showed this picture:

Table 1.2: The Total Outstanding Debt of Cultivators and Non-cultivators in Gijhi on June 30, 1925

	Borrowed from Agriculturist Moneylenders		*Borrowed from Non-Agriculturist Moneylenders*		*Total Debt*
	Amount	*Per cent*	*Amount*	*Per cent*	
1. Cultivators (68 owners and 10 non-owners)	9,730	32.56	20,149	67.44	29,879
2. Non-Cultivators (Non-cultivating owners- 43 persons)	7,680	40.49	11,288	59.51	18,968
Total	17,410	35.64	31,437	64.36	48,847

Source: BEIP, *An Economic Survey of Gijhi in Rohtak District*, 1932, p. 98.

65. *Report of the Punjab Provincial Banking Enquiry Committee, 1929-30*, Vol. 1, Lahore, 1930, p. 12.
66. Ibid., p. 132.
67. Ibid., p. 139.

Table 1.3: The Amount of Money Borrowed During the Year Ending June 30, 1925 in Gijhi

	Borrowed from Agriculturist Moneylenders		*Borrowed from Non-Agriculturist Moneylenders*		*Total Debt*
	Amount	*Per cent*	*Amount*	*Per cent*	
	Rs.		Rs.		Rs.
Cultivators	2,927	35.96	5,213	64.04	8,140
Non-Cultivators	1,166	33.87	2,276	66.13	3,442
Total	4,093	35.34	7,489	64.66	11,582

Source: BEIP, *An Economic Survey of Gijhi in Rohtak District*, 1932, p. 99.

These figures show that non-agriculturist moneylenders had a firm hold in the moneylending business: 64.36 per cent of the total debt and 64.66 per cent of the year's debt was still due to them.

Table 1.4: Debts Incurred by Owners and Tenants of Bhadas in 1930

Rate of interest per annum	*Sources*				
	Govern-ment	*Cooperative Society*	*Non-Agriculturist*	*Agri-culturist*	*Total*
	Rs.	*Rs.*	*Rs.*	*Rs.*	*Rs.*
Free ..	..	..	50	2,285	2,335
6 ¼ ..	4,667	..	..	..	4,667
12..	..	..	745	..	745
12 ½ ..	..	2,896	..	..	2,896
18 ¾ ..	..	..	100	..	100
24..	..	..	17,762	1,148	18,910
25..	..	..	..	60	60
28 1/8 ..	..	..	175	..	175
37 ½ ..	..	..	60	30	90
Total..	4,667	2,896	18,892	3,523	29,978
Percentage	15.5	9.7	63.0	11.8	100.0

Source: BEIP, *An Economic Survey of Bhadas in Gurgaon District 1936*, p. 74, Table 35.

According to the above figures the non-agriculturist moneylenders had lent out to cultivators about five times as much as agriculturist moneylenders. The increase of debt to the non-agriculturists may be due to the hard times which had set in at times of the resurvey.

There were various factors which contributed to this widespread indebtedness. Agriculture depended largely on the rains and the failure of rains was a common phenomenon in Haryana. The disastrous effects of the recurrent famines on the rural economy had been noted.[68] Insecurity of harvest also contributed in a big way in increasing the burden of debt. During the bad harvest, the peasant had to borrow for anything he wanted.[69] The major portion of the total debt of cultivators and non-cultivators was incurred in years of scarcity. A study of the mortgages shows that a fair portion of these can be traced back to 1905-06 and 1908-09 which were years of scarcity.[70] Small peasants borrowed at times as they were unable to save enough to meet unforeseen calamities.[71] The rise in the prices of agricultural products had reduced to abject poverty, the small owners, the tenants and the lower castes, who were obliged to purchase food-grains for their consumption. If they wanted a pair of shoes they went to moneylenders to borrow two rupees for the purpose, all their purchases and expenditure requiring cash were made with borrowed money. Small peasants grew crops only to hand over the produce to their creditors and then borrow again for their personal consumption.[72] After handing over the produce to the moneylenders the small

68. Himadri Banerjee, *Agrarian Society of the Punjab (1849-1901)*, New Delhi, 1982, p. 105.
69. Inderjit Sharma, *Land Revenue Administration in the Punjab (1849-1901)*, New Delhi, 1985, p. 158.
70. BEIP, *An Economic Survey of Gijhi in the Rohtak District*, 1932, p. 105.
71. H. Calvert, op. cit., p. 261.
72. BEIP, op. cit., p. 106

peasants had to borrow again for food grains. In this way the cycle of indebtedness continued.

Table 1.5: Classifying Indebtedness of Naggal Village According to Causes of Debt

Causes	*Amount (percentage)*
Family Expenses	4.2
Professional	5.3
Marriage	8.5
Old Debts	37.0
Business	13.0
Advances	32.0
Total	100.0

Source: BEIP, *An Economic Survey of Naggal in Ambala District*, 1933, p. 65, Table XXXIV.

The above table shows that the largest amount of borrowing was due to repayment of the 'old debt', 37 per cent of the total amount borrowed; 'advances' come next at 32 per cent; followed by 'business' and 'professional' expenses, together 18.3 per cent; marriage 8.5 and 'family expenses' 4.2. The 'advances' constitute money paid by the agriculturists to the whole time labourers working under them.

A village survey of Gijhi in Rohtak district describes poverty as the main reason for indebtedness:

> Indebtedness in Gijhi in the great majority of cases is due to poverty, not increased prosperity of the total number of owners (119), 29 own 8 or more than 5 acres in Gijhi. Of these, 11 are in debt, and the others are wholly free from debt. Of the smaller owners (less than 5 acres, 90 in number) 71.1 per cent are in debt as compared with 37.9 per cent of the larger owner (5 or more than 5 acres). It is evident then that a much higher proportion of the poorer cultivators than of the more prosperous owners are in debt. Cultivators whose principal dependence is not on agriculture borrow heavily for food.[73]

73. Ibid., p. 106.

As stated above poor peasants had to borrow to meet consumption demands and the substantial peasants borrowed money for ceremonial expenses or for purchase of land, bullocks and seeds. These were essential items for sustaining production and for the reproduction of the household.[74]

Table 1.6: Causes of Debt Outstanding in Bhadas in December 1930

Causes of Debt	*Amount (Rs.)*	*Percent to Total*
Payment of land leases and land revenue	2,519	8.4
Taking land on mortgage	1,225	4.1
Purchase of land	500	1.7
Redemption of land	830	2.8
Purchase of seed, cattle, fodder, and setting up Persian wheels (Rs. 130/-)	10,752	35.9
Building	1,000	3.3
Social observances	2,611	8.7
Litigations	–	
Living expenses	10,141	33.8
Miscellaneous (well-repairs Rs 150/-; inherited debt, Rs. 250/-)	400	1.3
Total	29,978	100.0

Source: BEIP, *An Economic Survey of Bhadas in Gurgaon District*, 1936, p. 75, Table 36.

The above figures show that the peasants borrowed maximum money for agricultural purposes such as purchase of seeds, cattle, fodder and setting up Persian wheels, etc.

The other cause of debt which is often exaggerated was the expenditure on domestic ceremonies on birth, marriage and death which were a necessary part of social life and

74. Neeladri Bhattacharya, 'Lenders and Debtors: Punjab Countryside, 1880-1940' in *Studies in History*, 1, 2, New Series, (1985) p. 338.

necessitated loans from moneylenders.[75] These were the occasions on which the poor got some respite from their dreary existence. The point is that the rural strata of rural society were so poor that they could not even meet these minimum social obligations from their resources.[76]

The peasants also borrowed from village cooperative societies. The main purposes of borrowing from these societies were repayment of old debts, redemption of mortgages and purchase of seeds and cattle. A survey of Bhadas shows:

Table 1.7: The Purposes of Borrowing from the Bhadas Co-operative Society

Purposes of Borrowing	*Amount (Rs.)*	*Percent to Total*
Repayment of old debts	2,175	29.6
Redemption of land	1,960	27.7
Purchase of seeds	71	1.0
Purchase of animals	290	4.1
Payment of land revenue	84	1.2
Purchase of animals and seeds	1,668	23.6
For more than one purpose: purchase of animals, seeds and payment of land revenue	910	12.8
Total	7,078	100.0

Source: BEIP, *An Economic Survey of Bhadas in Gurgaon District,* 1936, p. 77, Table 38.

The peasants repaid their debts by sale of cattle and surplus produce. But most of time, this was not sufficient. They had to mortgage their land. They had to borrow again for repayment of old debts and redemption of their land. In this way the process of indebtedness was continued.

75. Mridula Mukherhee, *Colonializing Agriculture: The Myth of Punjab Exceptionalism,* New Delhi, 2005, p. 43
76. Ibid.

III. RURAL RELATIONSHIP

In the Haryana region of colonial Punjab relations between various sections of rural society were noted as being strained. All these changes were the result of changes in the agrarian economy. Factors like the recording of proprietary rights, introduction of tenancy legislations and other Acts, increasing cultivation of commercial crops, steady rise in land value and growing competition for the acquisition of land among the various sections of the rural society complicated the agrarian scene.

The advent of British rule, the old village system of barter gradually gave way to a money economy.[77] Prior to the introduction of British rule the village servants like Tarkhans, Lohars, Chamars and Chuhras used to render manifold services to the proprietary body in connection with agriculture and received wages in kind when the harvest was over. Their wages were determined by the nature of their service and they were paid out of the common heap of produce. This traditional form of payment was gradually replaced by annual contracts and they were paid in cash for their job. But due to lack of agricultural prosperity in the Haryana region these agricultural labourers had to survive in a poor economic condition.[78]

Owing to poverty and agrarian backwardness, the relations between moneylenders and peasants, peasant proprietors and the tenants, peasants and the agricultural labourers were strained. Moneylenders were molested or murdered by the debtors[79] and clashes between the peasant

77. M.L. Darling, *The Punjab Peasant in Prosperity and Debt*, Columbia, 1925, p. 209.
78. Himadri Banerjee, 'Changes in Agrarian Society in the Late Nineteenth Century' in *Five Punjabi Centuries: Polity, Economy, Society and Culture, C. 1500-1900*, edited by Indu Banga, New Delhi, 1997, pp. 339-340.
79. Prem Chowdhry, Rural Relations Prevailing in the Punjab at the Time of Enactment of the So-called 'Golden Laws' or

proprietors and agricultural labourers were noted. Dacoities were reported. The economic conditions were largely responsible.[80]

Other reasons like communal propaganda and rivalry were also responsible for this situation. But in welcome contrast there were also examples of generosity shown by the sahukars. In Bhiwani of Haryana region the relations were most friendly between the sahukars and the peasants. The local mahajan showed generosity by providing large quantities of free fodder for the peasants' cattle during the time of scarcity and 70 to 75 per cent of cultivators could not repay their loans for lack of funds.[81]

In Haryana mostly peasants were small peasant proprietors. They owned a small size of land, i.e. five acres or less than five acres. The hardworking peasants did agriculture work on their own. However their income often fell short of consumption needs because they had to pay the land revenue and the debt which they borrowed to pay it. The labourers borrowed money from the moneylenders for food. Therefore due to poverty the relations between various sections of the society became strained. But there were also examples of mutual cooperation among the rural people in times of scarcity. Poverty, land revenue and agricultural backwardness were mainly responsible for the adverse condition of the peasants in Haryana.

Agrarian Legislations of the Late Thirties, in the *Punjab: Past and Present,* Vol. X – II, October 1976, pp. 476-477.

80. *Punjab Fortnightly Report (FR), First Half of October 1921,* F. No. 18 of 1921, NAI.
81. *Report of the Punjab Provincial Banking Enquiry Committee, 1929-30,* Vol. 1, Government Printing Press, Lahore, 1930, pp. 137-138.

2

Politicization of the Peasantry

The process of politicization of the peasantry in Haryana region had started after the introduction of the Montagu–Chelmsford Reforms of 1919. This Act divided the electorates in urban and rural areas. By this Act only candidates from 'agriculturist tribes' were allowed to fight the elections for the rural constituencies. Earlier the Government of India Act 1909 had divided the electorates on communal lines.

The Government of India Act of 1919 made changes in the structure and functioning of central and provincial legislatures. The Provincial Legislative Councils were enlarged and the majority of their members were to be elected. Under the system of Dyarchy the provincial governments were given more powers. Under this system some subjects, such as finance and law and order, were called reserved subjects and remained under the direct control of the Governor, others such as education, public health and local self-government were called 'transferred' subjects and were to be controlled by ministers responsible to the legislatures.[1]

Both for the provincial and central legislatures the voting qualifications were determined by age, education and ownership of property. Thus a major portion of India's population was barred from taking any part in the

1. Bipan Chandra, *Modern India,* NCERT, New Delhi, 1990, pp. 220-221.

constitution of the government.[2]

In 1920, the total number of voters at the centre was 909,874 for the lower house, the Legislative Assembly and 17,364 for the upper house, the Council of State. The lower house was to have 41 nominated members in a total strength of 144. The upper house was to have 26 nominated and 34 elected members.[3]

In the Punjab the strength of the legislative council was increased to 94 members, 23 nominated and 71 elected. The former were nominated by the Governor after seeking the approval of the Governor General.[4]

The property or status qualifications of a Punjab Legislative Council voter in 1920 were:[5]

(a) In Rural Constituencies

- (i) Owner/tenant/lessee of land assessed to land revenue not less than Rs. 25 p.a.
- (ii) Zaildar/Safedposh/Lambardar.
- (iii) Income tax payee.
- (iv) Retired (pensioned/discharged) officer o.r. of HM's regular forces.
- (v) Possessing qualifications of an urban voter.

(b) In Urban Constituencies

- (i) Owner/tenant of immovable property not being land, assessed to land revenue but including any building, etc. on it of the value of not less than Rs. 4,000 or of rental value of not less than Rs. 96 p.a.

---

2. *Indian Statutory Commission Volume XVI, Selection from Memoranda and Oral Evidence by Non-Officials (Part-1)*, London 1930, p. 79.
3. Bipan Chandra, op.cit., p. 221.
4. K.C. Yadav, *Elections in Punjab, 1920-47*, Delhi, 1987, p. 10.
5. *Punjab Government Gazette, Extraordinary*, August 7, 1920, cited in K.C. Yadav, op.cit., Delhi, 1987, p. 14.

(ii) Payee of muns. or cantt. tax amounting to not less than Rs. 50 p.a.
(iii) Income tax payee.
(iv) Retired (pensioned or discharged) officer/n.c.o/ soldier of HM's regular forces.
(v) Possessing qualifications of a rural voter.

(c) In Special Constituencies

Landholders' Constituencies—Owner of land assessed to land revenue not less than Rs. 500 p.a.

Punjab University Constituencies—Fellow/Hony. fellow/ graduate of the university of not less than 7 years standing.

Industries Constituencies—Owner or representative/ partner of a factory in Punjab or corporation with a paid up capital of Rs. 25,000.

Chamber of Commerce Constituencies—Member of the Chamber in Punjab.

The qualifications and restrictions mentioned above deterred the general masses from enrolling as voters. Hardly a little over 3 per cent population was enfranchised in the Punjab at that time. Thus the basis of franchise was very narrow and the vast bulk of the population went unrepresented.

The division of electorates on communal lines worsened the situation in Punjab. The separation of three communities into three water-tight compartments (Hindu, Muslim and Sikh) had divided the province into three hostile groups. During the elections there had always been a strong desire on the part of the candidates and their supporters to give communal colour to their speeches and election manifestos. This state of affairs had brought into prominence communal leaders, who, in order to gain political importance and wield political power inflamed the religious passions of the ignorant voters.[6]

6. *Indian Statutory Commission*, op.cit., p. 87.

In this way the division of the electorate on communal lines further spread communalism in India. By this the forces of nationalism and unity among Indians were disturbed and weakened.[7]

With the spread of representative politics into the province the British created separate electorates for the urban and rural areas. The reason was given that the new Legislative Council favoured the rural people because the seats were distributed proportionate to their population.[8] But they imposed restrictions on the rural masses whom had to fulfil the qualifications laid down for a voter.

The rural people, mostly peasants and agricultural labourers, were economically backward because of poverty, backwardness of agriculture, exploitation of peasants by moneylenders, merchants, capitalists and the colonial government and its officials.[9]

In the 1920s in the Punjab there was a rise in the nationalist and anti-British feelings among the urban people because of the nationalist movement. It also endeavoured to win over the agriculturist classes of the province which formed the backbone of the Indian Army.[10] Therefore the British wanted to separate the rural and urban population and made an effort to keep them away from the influence of the nationalist movement. So, in the Punjab a further division in the electorate on a rural and urban basis was introduced within the communal division.

As a result, a party who was first called the Rural Bloc, then the Rural Party and later the Punjab National Unionist

---

7. K.C. Yadav, op.cit., p. 5.
8. I.A. Talbot, 'Deserted Collaborators: The Political Background to the Rise and Fall of the Punjab Unionist Party, 1923-1947', in the *Journal of Imperial and Commonwealth History*, Vol. XI, October 1982, No. 1, p. 77.
9. See Chapter 1.
10. *Punjab FR First Half of January 1920*, F. No. 78, and *Punjab FR Second Half of August 1920*, F. No. 112, NAI.

Party with a pro-agriculturist ideology formally emerged in 1923. Fazl-i-Husain who had parted company with the Congress and Khilafatists when they adopted the policy of Non-Cooperation was elected to the Punjab Legislative Council in 1921 and was appointed a minister under the new scheme of dyarchy. In the second council, the Unionist Party was able to command a majority and get two of its members appointed as ministers, one being Fazl-i-Husain and the other Lal Chand, a Jat agriculturist from Rohtak district in Haryana. But Lal Chand was later disqualified because of an election petition and Chaudhri Chhotu Ram another Jat agriculturist from Rohtak, was appointed in his place and he rose as the most important non-Muslim leader of the Unionist Party. The Congress was split between the Swarajists who wanted to contest elections and the no-changers who did not, and the Swarajists were therefore unable to bring the whole weight of the Congress to bear on their electoral mobilization.[11]

In other words, the Congress was split between the Swarajists popularly known as 'pro-changers' who wanted to enter the councils and 'no-changers' who were advocating boycott of the councils. The Swarajists wanted to transform the legislatures into arenas of political struggle and to use them as the ground on which the struggle for the overthrowal of the colonial state was to be carried out. The no-changers opposed council-entry mainly on the ground that parliamentary work led to the neglect of constructive work among the masses.[12]

The position of the Unionists was no longer as strong as it had been in the second council from 1924-26 and this had

11. Mridula Mukherjee, *Peasants in India's Non-Violent Revolution: Practice and Theory*, New Delhi, 2004, pp. 37-38.
12. Bipan Chandra et. al., *India's Struggle for Independence*, Delhi, 1989, p. 237.

predictable effects on the unity of the party.[13] In 1926, the Governor of the Punjab, Sir Malcom Hailey, again revived the principle of communal representation with a view to break the solidarity of the Unionists. While Feroz Khan Noon replaced Fazl-i-Husain as minister, as his colleague the Governor appointed Lala Manohar Lal, dropping Chaudhri Chhotu Ram. He also gave separate representation to the Sikhs by including Sir Joginder Singh in the ministry.[14] In this way the Governor appointed the ministers on communal grounds. In the next elections of 1930 the strength of the Unionists diminished and the government again conceded only one minister to the party.[15] As Fazl-i-Husain was appointed a member of the Viceroy's Executive Council in 1930, an agriculturist Sikander Hyat Khan was appointed in his place. Although the Unionist Party lost some of its power, it nevertheless exerted a dominant and moderating influence on provincial politics throughout the period 1923-37.[16] In other words, the influence of the Unionist Party increased.

In 1937, there were again elections in the Punjab. The Congress, the Nationalist Party, the Unionist Party and other parties fielded their candidates for the constituencies in Ambala division. The Congress formed an Election Board with its headquarters at Rohtak. Shri Ram Sharma was placed in charge of the Board. The Unionist Party made Chaudhri Chhotu Ram in charge of its election campaign. Rao Balbir Singh led the campaigning for the Hindu Mahasabha candidates.[17]

The Congress started its campaign in a big way. Eminent

---

13. Ibid., p. 39.
14. D.C. Verma, *Haryana,* New Delhi, 1990, pp. 36-37.
15. Mridula Mukherjee, op.cit., p. 39.
16. I.A. Talbot, *op.cit.,* pp. 78-79.
17. Jagdish Chander, 'Political Development in Haryana, 1928-1947', in *Haryana: Studies in History and Politics,* edited by J.N. Singh Yadav, New Delhi, 1976, p. 120.

leaders visited the region. Mrs. Sarojini Naidu addressed election meetings at Ambala, Shahabad, Karnal, Panipat, Kaithal, Rohtak, Hissar and Jagadhri.[18] At Ambala she said, "The Congress stood for justice, equity and fair deal to all classes and sects. It stands for equal opportunities to both men and women. It is an equal well-wisher of the kisans, mahajans, villagers and the town people".[19] Pandit Jawaharlal Nehru addressed meetings in Ambala, Karnal and Rohtak districts. He held the government responsible for all the people's present ills—poverty, unemployment and lack of national freedom. Almost every speech ended with an electioneering appeal for the support of Congress candidates and it was urged that only the Congress had the will and the capacity to face the task before the country.[20] He stressed everywhere the view that no improvement in the state of the country was possible under British imperialism, the present British government had, therefore, to be turned out and the Congress was the only organization in India capable of doing this, therefore it should be supported.[21] In this way Pandit Nehru criticized the colonial government and held it responsible for all the misery of the Indian people.

Fazl-i-Husain and Chaudhri Chhotu Ram toured all over Haryana canvassing support for the Unionist candidates. In villages, especially in Rohtak district, the two leaders were received with great honour and enthusiasm from the peasants.[22] In its election manifesto the Unionist Party promised many measures for the amelioration of the peasants and education of the rural people.[23] The Unionist

18. Ibid.
19. *The Tribune,* January 6, 1937, p. 4, C.2.
20. *Punjab FR First Half of August 1936,* F. No. 18/8/1936, NAI.
21. *Punjab FR Second Half of January 1937,* F. No. 18/1/1937, NAI.
22. Jagdish Chander, op.cit., p. 121.
23. Madan Gopal, *Sir Chhotu Ram: The Man and the Vision,* Ghaziabad, 1997, p. 60.

Party also claimed that "It is the only party capable of fulfilling its undertakings because it is the only party that can be returned in a sufficiently large majority to form a stable government. No other party is in that position."[24] By this Unionists became popular among the peasants and the rural masses.

Raja Narender Nath and Rao Balbir Singh, the Hindu Mahasabha leaders toured the constituencies to support the candidates. They appealed to the voters to cast their votes in the name of Hinduism and for its protection and progress. Pandit Madan Mohan Malviya toured the area asking the electorate to vote for candidates of the Nationalist Party.[25] But these parties could not gain the support of the peasantry.

After these elections, the Unionist Party emerged as the most powerful single party in Haryana. It got twelve out of twenty-two seats.[26] All Congress candidates from rural constituencies of the Ambala division were defeated with the exception of Lala Duni Chand who won the Ambala (rural) constituency.[27] However, all the Congress candidates in urban constituencies were successful.[28] The election results showed that the Unionist Party had a strong rural base while the Congress Party was popular among the urban people in Haryana.

In the Punjab Legislative Assembly out of 175 seats, the Unionists won 99 seats with a clear majority, Congress won 18, Khalsa Nationalist Party got 13, Hindu Mahasabha won 12, Akali won 11, Ahrars won 2, Ittihad Millat won 2, Muslim League won 1, Congress Nationalist won 1 seat and Independents got 16 seats.[29]

---

24. *The Tribune,* January 17, 1937, p. 1, C.1.
25. Jagdish Chander, op.cit., p. 121.
26. Ibid., p. 122.
27. *Punjab FR First Half of February 1937,* F. No. 18/2/1937, NAI.
28. *Punjab FR Second Half of February 1937,* F. No. 18/2/1937, NAI.
29. Jagdish Chander, op.cit., p. 123.

Sikandar Hyat Khan became the premier of the Punjab. Dr. Sunder Singh Majithia, Minister of Revenue, Mr. Manohar Lal—Finance Minister, Major Khizar Hyat Khan Tiwana—Minister of Public Works, Mian Abdul Haye—Minister of Education and from Haryana Chaudhri Chhotu Ram became Development Minister.[30]

In the elections of 1937, the Unionist success in the rural electorates was the result of projecting their agrarian programmes as aimed at solving the economic difficulties of peasants. These policies enabled the Unionist Party to sweep the board in both the Muslim and Hindu rural constituencies of the Haryana region.[31] These results also indicated the hold of the Unionists on the peasantry. The Congress organization was divided against itself and the internal dissensions was one of the main reasons for the failure of the Congress in the Punjab.[32] Another important reason for the defeat of the Congress Party in the election of 1937 in the Punjab was its inability to reach the peasantry. Pandit Jawaharlal Nehru, the President of the All India Congress Committee analysed the situation and wrote to Dr. Gopi Chand Bhargava:

> I must confess that I have not quite got over the fact that the key seats in the Punjab were left uncontested by us. It is my belief that we have captured almost every rural seat in the Punjab, Hindu, Muslim, or Sikh, if we had approached the peasantry on the right lines.
>
> The Congress does not even go near the peasantry in the Punjab and in cities it is busy with personal squabbles.[33]

The Unionists were able to maintain their hold over the Punjab till 1945. The next elections were held in 1946 after

---

30. *Punjab Legislative Assembly Debates, 1937-46,* NMML.
31. I.A. Talbot, op.cit., p. 79.
32. *Punjab FR Second Half of June 1936,* F. No. 18/6/1936, NAI.
33. Letter, Pandit Jawaharlal Nehru to Dr. Gopi Chand Bhargava, March 5, 1937, *Gopi Chand Bhargava Papers*, Correspondence with Jawaharlal Nehru, p. 8, NMML.

the end of the Second World War. In the Punjab Legislative Assembly elections of 1946, the Muslim League won the majority of seats, i.e. out of 175 it got 75, Congress won 51, Akalis got 22, and the Unionists won 20, and 7 seats went to independent candidates. The election represents a gain of 53 seats for the League and of 18 seats for the Congress. The Communists lost the four seats which they held previously. Fifty-seven Unionist Muslims were unseated.[34] In the Haryana region Congress fared well, i.e. out of 21 seats it won 11 seats, six seats went to the Muslim League and four to the Unionists.[35]

In general rural constituencies, 'the most notable defeat' of the 1946 elections in the 'citadel of Hindu Unionists' was that of Tika Ram, the political successor of Chaudhri Chhotu Ram, the unrivalled leader of this region from 1923 to 1945, who had served as the Revenue Minister and also the Parliamentary Secretary from 1937 to 1945. The Jhajjar constituency which had given a massive victory to Chaudhri Chhotu Ram was lost to a Congress candidate.[36] This seat had been won by Chaudhri Chhotu Ram in 1937 by a majority of votes, and after his death, his nephew was elected from the same constituency.

The Congress had been paying special attention to the untouchables and agricultural labourers right from the 1920s. The Congress took up the forced labour issue and got the support of the untouchables by promising to save them from forced labour both to the landowners and the government officials.[37] Basically during this time the Nationalist Movement was successful in the countryside and therefore the Congress Party was successful in Haryana.

---

34. *Punjab FR Second Half of February 1946*, F. No. 18/2/1946, NAI.
35. Jagdish Chander, op.cit., p. 140.
36. *The Tribune*, February 21, 1946, p. 1.
37. Prem Chowdhry, 'The Congress Triumph in South-East Punjab: Elections of 1946', *Studies in History*, Vol. II, No. 2 (1980), p. 84.

During and after the Second World War the voters shifted their allegiance elsewhere for many reasons. The main event responsible for this shift was the rise of the Indian National Army (INA). A large number of INA personnel belonged to the Punjab. The Punjab Provincial Congress Committee was quick to take up their cause. By supporting the INA cause, the Congress increased its social base. The Congress took up two major issues in the elections—repression of 1942 and the trials of the INA prisoners.[38] The Congress organization had been seriously considering the question of finding employment and financial relief for INA personnel.[39]

In order to deal with the INA problem, the Congress set up relief and employment committees in each of the five districts of this region. After their release the INA personnel began to contact the Congress organization and attend Congress meetings. Many of them got enrolled as Congress workers and became Congress election propagandists.[40] In this way the Congress Party got the support and services of these people.

For the election campaign, many central and Punjab Congress leaders visited Haryana and addressed election meetings at various places. On behalf of the Congress, Sarat Chandra Bose visited this region. He observed in a public meeting at Hissar that "in 1942 India as a nation rose against the foreign rule. Gandhiji inspired the whole country with his two words 'Quit India'. Indians in Burma and Malaya took to arms, formed the INA under the leadership of Netaji Subhas Chandra Bose and made an attempt to give practical shape to Gandhiji's words". He started his election campaign and addressed eighteen meetings in villages and small towns

---

38. Sucheta Mahajan, *Independence and Partition*, New Delhi, 2000, p. 79.
39. *Punjab FR First Half of February 1946*, F. No. 18/2/1946, NAI.
40. See *FR of the Punjab between July 1945 to February* 1946, NAI.

of Rohtak district carrying the Congress message to more than one lakh people. He also addressed public meetings at Bhiwani, Sirsa, Hissar and many other places.[41]

He said that the Congress participation in the elections was not an isolated thing. It was part and parcel of the national struggle for freedom and the elections of today were a continuation of the Quit India Movement and of the sacrifices of the INA.[42] In this way these three things, viz. the Quit India Movement, INA trials and the elections were interlinked by the nationalists as an election agenda. Voting for Congress was equal to voting for freedom.

Pandit Jawaharlal Nehru also visited Rohtak, Gurgaon, Hissar, Karnal and Panipat districts. He was accompanied by Pandit Neki Ram Sharma and Pandit Shri Ram Sharma during his tour of the Haryana Prant.[43] He addressed about twenty-four public meetings. "The cry of religion in danger", said Pandit Nehru, "was the outcome of the existence of British Imperialism in India. As soon as this third party leaves India bag and baggage, India would stand united as never before. This is what 'Quit India' means. The soundness of this slogan has been amply proved by the communal unity maintained by the soldiers of the INA while they were free from British influence."[44] In this way he made colonial rule responsible for present crisis in India.

Pandit Nehru also said, "The Congress decided to fight elections not to install itself in place of power and position but to prevent the undesirable and heterogeneous elements from occupying the representative position and to show that the bulk of India's population was one with the Congress in its demand for complete independence."[45] He also remarked,

41. *The Tribune*, January 4, 1946, p. 1.
42. Ibid.
43. *The Tribune*, January 30, 1946, p. 10, C.3.
44. Ibid.
45. Ibid.

"I would not hesitate even to take arms, if that remains the only way to attain India's independence. But non-violence under the circumstances is a better and more effective weapon to win this end."[46] Thus Congress wanted complete independence of India by way of non-violence only.

However, the Punjab Congress at this time, was structurally weak, disorganized, divided and faction-ridden. The resignation of Mian Iftikhar-ud-din, president of the Punjab Provincial Congress Committee, from the Congress to join the Muslim League at this juncture, came as a big blow to the Congress.[47] The division of the Punjab Congress into two groups and shift of the leaders from Congress to the Muslim League weakened its position in the Punjab.

The factional struggle between the groups of Gopi Chand Bhargava and Satyapal further weakened the position of the Punjab Congress. Maulana Abul Kalam Azad, President of the Indian National Congress, came to Punjab, talked to the various groups of the Congress and to a large extent succeeded in effecting a compromise among the various groups. He appointed Maulana Daud Ghaznavi as President of the Punjab Provincial Congress Committee.[48] Although the Punjab Congress was again divided on the issue of its attitude towards the Akalis, some of the leaders of the Provincial Congress wanted an election compromise with the Akalis, whereas others were against any compromise.[49] In this way, the central leadership had to interfere in the provincial matters.

The important features of the Congress election propaganda in the Punjab were the demand for the release of the Indian National Army personnel and the slogan of

46. Ibid.
47. *Punjab FR Second Half of September 1945*, F. No. 18/9/1945, NAI.
48. *Punjab FR Second Half of October 1945*, F. No. 18/10/1945, NAI.
49. *Punjab FR Second Half of December 1945*, F. No. 18/12/1945, NAI.

complete independence. This attitude of the Congress strengthened its position especially in Haryana. The war time grievances of the people such as high prices, shortages and economic controls alienated the Unionists' traditional supporters and led to the consolidation of the Congress.[50] In other words, the anti-incumbency factor was also beneficial for Congress in these elections.

The Unionist Party was another important political party which took part in the provincial elections of 1946. This party was no longer so active. Its great leaders Chaudhri Chhotu Ram and Sikander Hyat Khan were no more.[51] The road was clear for Jinnah who had been rebuffed first by Fazl-i-Husain and after his death by Chaudhri Chhotu Ram.[52]

At the Simla Conference in 1945, Mr. Jinnah asserted that the nomination of a Muslim to the Viceroy's Executive Council could be done only by the Muslim League with his consent and that any decision of the Executive Council to which the Muslims objected could only be carried by a two thirds majority of the council. These demands were not accepted by the Viceroy and Jinnah refused to cooperate with him. The conference had failed. After this Jinnah was able to establish finally that he and his party alone was the spokesman of the Muslims of India.[53] This conference further weakened the position of the Unionist Party in the Punjab.

The Unionist Party had also used government machinery for mobilizing the support of village voters. This damaged the reputation of the party which it had achieved during its early years in office. It depended greatly on the administrative resources, land grants, war front funds and

---

50. Prem Chowdhry, op.cit., pp. 103-105.
51. *Punjab Legislative Assembly Debate*, February 19, 1945, p. 6.
52. Deepak Pandey, 'The Social Base of Unionist Party', *Punjab History Conference*, 13th Session, March 1979, p. 283.
53. Raghuvendra Tanwar, *Politics of Sharing Power: The Punjab Unionist Party, 1923-47*, New Delhi, 1999, p. 175.

propaganda regarding the various agricultural reforms.[54] But the propaganda of the Unionists had no relevance and it became outdated at the time when the Congress Party had given the slogan of 'complete independence' and the Muslim League had demanded Pakistan.

The war time inflation and growing shortages of consumer goods such as cloth, iron, cement, sugar and kerosene which became virtually unobtainable in the villages brought considerable hardship to the rural people. The inflation also wiped out the profits which resulted from the increase of price of such crops as wheat, maize, gram and bajra. All these made the Unionist Party's position vulnerable in the Punjab.[55] The Muslim League made full use of this situation in the Punjab and made the Unionist Party responsible for all the peasants' economic problems.

The Unionist Party issued its manifesto which stressed the economic achievement of the ministry including the reduction of the agricultural debt by two crores of rupees. The stated aims of the Unionist Party were provincial autonomy, complete independence, free and compulsory primary education for the poor, and reduction in military expenditure.[56] But all this did not work in these elections.

The Unionists put forward the slogan of United Punjab and Punjabis in response to the Pakistan slogan of the Muslim League. The Unionists argued that the important issue for the voters was not Pakistan but the choice was between chaos, disorder and communal bitterness on the one side which was the only prospect held out by the Muslim League group and a stable and efficient administration offered by the Unionists.[57]

---

54. Ian Talbot, 'The 1946 Punjab Election,' *Modern Asian Studies*, 14, 1 (1980), p. 90.
55. Ian Talbot, *Punjab and the Raj (1849-1947)*, New Delhi, 1988, p. 144.
56. *Civil and Military Gazette*, November 29, 1945.
57. *The Tribune*, October 28, 1945.

Due to the war time economic dislocation the Unionist Party had also become unpopular amongst the small peasants in Haryana.[58] They suffered shortages of vital commodities such as cloth, sugar and kerosene. In the Ambala district there were constant complaints about rationing. Most of the supplies of kerosene never reached the villages.[59] All this made the peasants discontented and unhappy with the Unionists.

The onset of winter made this shortage in woollen cloth and fuel more acute, more so as there was no likelihood of supplies being increased. In fact the local and provincial press reported a 'cloth famine' in Ambala division.[60] The then Punjab Premier Sir Khizr Hyat Khan Tiwana had issued an appeal to the people urging them to cooperate with him and help him fully in meeting the critical food situation.[61] He made efforts to stop black-marketing which also intensified the misery.

However, this time the argument about the economic achievement of the Unionist Party and the call for inter-communal cooperation did not get a response from the Muslims of the Punjab. The Muslim League took advantage of the war time grievances. Now the demand for Pakistan became popular among them because the Muslim League propagated that Pakistan was the only solution to their socio-economic problems.[62]

In these elections the Muslim League was very active and several of its leaders visited the Muslim majority areas. Relations between the different communities were getting

---

58. The Unionist Party's powerbase was among the small peasant proprietors in Haryana.
59. I.A. Talbot, 'The 1946 Punjab Elections', *Modern Asian Studies*, 14, 1 (1980), pp. 72-73.
60. *The Tribune*, April 26, 1945, p. 6 and July 6, 1945, p. 5.
61. Ibid., February 22, 1946, p. 4, C.3.
62. Amarjit Singh, *Punjab Divided: Politics of Muslim League and Partition,1935-45*, New Delhi, 2001, pp. 139-140.

increasingly strained. The Deputy Commissioner of Ambala writes "increasing reports of deterioration in the communal situation consequent on the poisonous propaganda of political parties especially of the Muslim League are being received from rural areas. One very objectionable type of propaganda indulged in by the Muslim League is to threaten Muslim voters." Much the same thing happened in Lahore and other places. Cries of 'Jai Hind' were greeted with shouts of 'Pakistan'.[63] For the Muslim League 'Pakistan' was the main election agenda. In this way, to attain the victory and goal of Pakistan the Muslim League was prepared to cross all limits in the elections.

In Haryana the communal situation became tense. The line up at the elections had been mainly along party lines, Hindus siding with the Congress and Muslims with the League.[64] In the elections the Congress fared well in Haryana but, in Muslim majority areas of West Punjab, the Muslim League won the majority of seats. Owing to the spread of communalism in these elections the polarization of the communities took place.

After the 1937 elections, as a leader of the Muslim League Muhammed Ali Jinnah forged a pact with the then new Unionist Premier of the Punjab, Sir Sikandar Hyat Khan, by which Jinnah essentially recognized the authority of the Unionists in the Punjab politics in return for joining the Muslim League and supporting it at the all-India level.[65]

In 1944, Mr. Jinnah had talks with Khizr Hyat Khan Tiwana on the issue of the relationship between the Unionist Party and the Muslim League at both the national and provincial levels of politics. They talked on three proposals

---

63. *Transfer of Power,* Vol. VI, p. 807.
64. *Punjab FR First Half of February 1946,* F. No. 18/2/1946, NAI.
65. David Gilmartin, 'Religious Leadership and the Pakistan Movement in the Punjab', *Modern Asian Studies,* 13,3 (1979), p. 505.

and these were (1) that every member of the Muslim League Party in the Punjab Assembly should declare that he owes allegiance solely to the Muslim League Party in the Assembly and not to the Unionists or any other Party, (2) that the present label of the coalition, namely the "Unionist Party" should be dropped, (3) that the name of the proposed coalition should be Muslim League Coalition Party.[66]

But the talks finally broke down over Khizr's insistence that the new coalition ministry which would be created after the establishment of a Muslim League Assembly Party should retain the Unionist Party name. In the dispute the League denied that it had ever recognized the Jinnah-Sikander Pact of 1937. It resulted in Khizr's expulsion from the League.[67] The Muslim League's target was to break the Unionist Party. The League also wanted to mobilize the people on communal lines in these elections.

The provincial elections of 1946 were quite crucial for the Punjab Provincial Muslim League since it had to prove that the demand for Pakistan was popular in this key Muslim area. Pakistan and Islam were the main issues for the leaders of the Provincial Muslim League and after the failure of the Simla Conference these leaders had already launched a vigorous attack against the Unionist Party and begun to strengthen the cause of the League.[68] The Leaders of the Punjab Provincial Muslim League issued a statement against the attitude of Khizr Hyat Khan Tiwana at the Simla Conference and called him a traitor to Islam. This had a tremendous effect on the politics of the province. The Muslim League put all its effort to become the representative of all the Muslims of India as it did in the Simla Conference and in these elections it used all methods to get Muslim votes.

---

66. Ikram Ali Malik, *The History of Punjab, 1799-1947*, New Delhi, 1970, p. 569.
67. I.A. Talbot, op.cit., p. 70.
68. *Punjab FR Second Half of July 1945*, F. No. 18/7/1945, NAI.

The Unionist Party depended on local notables whose support was always a matter of calculation not commitment. When it became clear that the Muslim League would provide the benefit of the office in future, the rural notables from all sections began shifting their support from the Unionist Party to the Muslim League.[69]

The rural 'pirs' also supported the League's appeal for Pakistan. They used their local influence in "democratic" politics and their support also helped to neutralize religious opposition to Pakistan from many 'Ulema'. Thus they underlined the religious foundation of the Pakistan demand.[70]

The Muslim League's cry of Islam in danger and the slogan of Pakistan were gaining strength. In Lahore, a Muslim League workers' centre was established, where a batch of thirty to fifty workers would come and stay and have their training for a week and then would leave for the propaganda campaign. Jinnah's campaign in favour of Pakistan at the all India level was also arousing the Muslims of Punjab.[71]

The Tribune published an article under the heading 'Jinnah threatens civil war' with a reference to the *New York Times* on its front page. The correspondent said that Mr. Jinnah told him that "if the British carry out their intention of calling a single constitution making body the only result would be a Muslim revolt throughout India."[72]

In the election campaign the League workers also tried to exploit the war time grievances of the soldiers, who had begun to return to the province once the war was over.[73]

---

69. Amarjit Singh, op.cit., p. 150.
70. David Gilmartin, *Empire and Islam: Punjab and the Making of Pakistan*, Delhi, 1989, p. 215.
71. Amarjit Singh, op.cit., p. 152.
72. *The Tribune*, February 15, 1946, p. 3.
73. *The Tribune*, October 27, 1945.

Many grievances existed among servicemen on the eve of the elections, and unemployment was one of them. By the end of 1946 less than twenty per cent of the demobilized soldiers those who registered with employment exchanges had found work.[74]

The Muslim League established a defence committee for the Indian National Army members who were on trial and this was well received in the main recruiting districts.[75] The Muslim League by exploiting the war time grievances of the demobilized soldiers simply eroded the base of the Unionists in the main recruiting districts. Similarly, the Congress also exploited the war time grievances of the soldiers of Haryana and secured victory in this region in the elections of 1946.[76]

Both parties, the Congress and the Muslim League, had benefited from the INA issue. The Muslim League got the support of soldiers in West Punjab while the Congress was able to get their support in Haryana.

During the election campaign the Muslim League tried to exploit the religious sentiments of the people. The Muslim League in a poster asked Muslims to choose between 'Din' and 'Duniya', in the battle of rightness and falsehood.[77] The leaders of the Provincial Muslim League asked for support for the sake of their religion and those who opposed the League were condemned as infidels and the copies of the 'Holy Quran' were carried around as an emblem peculiar to the Muslim League.[78]

The Punjab Muslim Student Federation played an important role in mobilizing the Muslim voters in favour of the Muslim League. They gave the slogan 'now or never'

74. Ian Talbot, op.cit., pp. 75-76.
75. Ibid., p. 76.
76. Prem Chowdhry, op.cit., pp. 98-105.
77. David Gilmartin, *Empire and Islam: Punjab and the Making of Pakistan*, Delhi, 1989, p. 189.
78. Glancy to Wavell, February 28, 1946, see Anita Inder Singh, *The Origin of the Partition of India*, Delhi, 1987, pp. 133-134.

for the election campaign. Hundreds of Muslim students enrolled themselves as volunteers. The groups of students toured the villages of the Punjab. They also toured various villages of East Punjab districts including Rohtak, Ambala and Hissar. They addressed many small gatherings and explained the programme and aims of the Muslim League.[79] In this way, the propaganda of the Muslim League and the Punjab Muslim Students Federation put the Muslim League in a formidable position in the elections of 1946 in the Punjab.

The leaders of the different factions of the Akali and Nationalist 'Sikhs' also contested the elections. The anti-Pakistan feelings and the opposition of the Muslim League brought different Sikh leaders together and they decided to contest the elections under the banner of Panthic Sikhs.[80]

The Akali election campaign was marked by an anti-Pakistan and anti-Muslim League slant. Master Tara Singh had declared that he would oppose the formation of a Muslim League ministry in the Punjab tooth and nail, because the Panth was not prepared to permit those elements to strengthen themselves which wanted the Punjab to be separated from the country.[81] The Akalis, like the Congress, fully utilized the issue of the Indian National Army personnel during their election campaigns.[82] Thus the Panthic Sikhs consolidated their position in the central Punjab. Other political parties such as the Communists, the Ahrars, the Khaksars and the Hindu Mahasabha also contested the elections but with little success.

Though in the elections of 1946 in the Punjab the Muslim League got seventy-five seats, still it was not in a clear majority and as such it could not form a ministry. A coalition

---

79. Amarjit Singh, op.cit., p. 159.
80. *Transfer of Power*, Vol. VI, p. 93.
81. *The Tribune*, February 24, 1946, p. 4.
82. *Punjab FR Second Half of November 1945*, F. No. 18/11/1945, NAI.

of the Congress, the Unionists and the Akalis formed the ministry. Khizr Hyat Khan became Chief Minister. The ministry however did not function properly because the Muslim League did not allow it to proceed with business.[83] Muslim League pressed hard for a 'separate nation'.[84]

Thus, we see that in the elections held between 1920 and 1946 in the Punjab various political parties played different roles. The Punjab National Unionist Party which emerged in 1923 formed a government under provincial autonomy in 1937 and ruled till 1946. The Muslim League which was very weak in the Punjab got a formidable position in 1946 by winning a large number of seats in the elections. The Congress Party consolidated its position in the Punjab particularly in Haryana, as did the Akalis in Central Punjab. Other political parties such as the Communists, the Ahrars, the Khaksars and the Hindu Mahasabha were also present, but not powerful.

---

83. Jagdish Chander, op.cit., p.141.
84. *Punjab Legislative Assembly Debates*, March 1946, p. 166, March 23, 1946.

3

Peasants in the National Movement

I

The Indian National Congress started the Non-Cooperation Movement in 1920 against the imperial rule. It adopted the following resolution which spelt out different items of the programme:

(i) The surrender of titles, honorary offices and nominated seats on local bodies.
(ii) Refusal to attend government levees, darbars, officials and semi-official functions.
(iii) The gradual withdrawal of children from schools and colleges owned, aided or controlled by government and the establishment of national schools and colleges in the different provinces in place of those maintained by government.
(iv) Gradual boycott by lawyers and litigants of British courts and the establishment of private arbitration courts for the settlement of private disputes.
(v) Refusal on the part of the military, clerical and labouring classes to offer as recruits for service in Mesopotamia.
(vi) Withdrawal by candidates of candidature for elections and refusal on the part of voters to vote for any candidate who may offer himself for election.
(vii) Boycott of foreign goods.[1]

1. *Punjab FR, First Half of September 1920*, F. No. 113, NAI.

After the adoption of the non-cooperation resolution, Gandhiji along with the Ali brothers started a nation-wide tour during which he addressed hundreds of meetings.[2] As a part of the boycott of educational institutions, thousands of students left schools and colleges and joined more than 800 national schools and colleges that had sprung up all over the country.[3] The educational boycott was particularly successful in Bengal but other areas were also active. Punjab, too responded to the educational boycott.[4] This movement was also popular in Haryana.

Many conferences were held in Haryana to support the Khilafat and Non-Cooperation movement. In Bhiwani a conference was held between 22nd and 24th October 1920. The speeches were delivered by Gandhiji, Muhammad Ali and Shaukat Ali. Among other prominent leaders who attended the conference were Abdul Kalam Azad, Dr. M.A. Ansari, Neki Ram Sharma and Swami Satyadeva.[5]

The District and Khilafat conference was also held in Rohtak in the first half of October 1920. Anti-government speeches were delivered, and, on the third day of the conference, the non-cooperation resolution was passed.[6] On November 30, 1920, a mass meeting was also held in Bhiwani attended by more than six thousand people. All the students who had left the schools were present. The meeting dispersed with thundering cries of "Mahatma Gandhi ki jai".[7]

As part of the boycott of British courts, many leading lawyers of the country, such as C.R. Das, Motilal Nehru, M.R. Jayakar, Saifuddin Kitchlew, Vallabhbhai Patel,

---

2. Bipan Chandra et al., *India's Struggle for Independence*, New Delhi, 1998, p. 187.
3. Ibid.
4. Ibid.
5. *Punjab FR, Second Half of October 1920*, F. No. 66, NAI.
6. *Punjab FR, First Half of October 1920*, F. No. 74, NAI.
7. *The Tribune*, December 2, 1920, p. 2, C.2.

C. Rajgopalachari, T. Prakasan and Asaf Ali gave up lucrative practices.[8] The same thing happened in Haryana. Duni Chand of Ambala gave up his practice at the High Court at Lahore. Abdul Rashid, Gulam Bhik and Durga Charan did the same in Ambala. Sham Lal left his practice in Hissar. His friends and followers also followed him. Sham Lal of Rohtak, and Ram Chander Vaid, Dwarka Das, Abdul Majid and Jugal Kishore of Karnal also did the same.[9] In Panipat, panchayats started to dispose of petty cases without resort to the courts.[10] The litigants also boycotted the government courts. The cases were taken to national courts, one of which was at Bhiwani.[11]

In January 1921, Lala Lajpat Rai started a campaign to boycott educational institutions in Rohtak.[12] Many schools and colleges including the Hindu School of Sonipat, the Jat and Vaishya Schools, Rohtak, disaffiliated themselves from Punjab University.[13]

Gandhiji visited Bhiwani, Kalanaur and Rohtak and addressed the large crowds.[14] In Bhiwani, on February 15, 1921, Gandhiji along with Mrs. Gandhi, Maulana Abul Kalam Azad, Lala Pyari Lal and others addressed large crowds of 30,000 people. Gandhiji also addressed a ladies meeting and at the end thousands came forth with rupees, rings, ornaments and bangles for the national cause. In this meeting ten thousand ladies were present.[15]

---

8. Bipan Chandra et al., op.cit., p. 187.
9. K.C. Yadav, *Modern Haryana: History and Culture, 1803-1966*, New Delhi, 2002, p. 169.
10. *Punjab FR, Second Half of December 1920*, F. No. 77, NAI.
11. K.C. Yadav, op.cit., p. 169.
12. *Punjab FR, Second Half of January 1921*, F. No. 42, NAI.
13. K.C. Yadav, 'The Struggle for Freedom: Haryana, 1885-1947', *Journal of Haryana Studies*, Vol. XXVII-XXVIII, 1995-1996, Kurukshetra University, Kurukshetra, Haryana, p. 65.
14. *Punjab FR, Second Half of February 1921*, F. No. 43, N.A.I.
15. *The Tribune*, February 18, 1921, p. 4, C.4.

During the Non-Cooperation Movement, meetings were held in most districts. These meetings promoted the programme of mass enrolment of Congress workers, the collection of funds and the distribution of spinning wheels.[16] The anti-liquor campaign was also successful in the province.[17]

In January 1922, in Hissar and Rohtak, there were a number of demonstrations and processions by volunteers accompanied by a large number of people. Police dispersed the crowds and arrested many leaders. Lala Lajpat Rai and other leaders were sentenced to one year's rigorous imprisonment.[18] Pandit Shri Ram Sharma was also jailed for one year.[19]

In most of the districts there had been picketing of liquor and foreign cloth shops. In Karnal pickters were marched off for prosecution.[20] In Rohtak district there was a disturbance at a village fair where the confectioners' shops were looted and damaged on the ground that they were using foreign sugar.[21] Except for this small incident the overall movement in Haryana was peaceful.

The incident at Chauri Chaura in Gorakhpur district of UP led to the end of the Non-Cooperation Movement, where on February 5, 1922, irritated by the behaviour of some policemen, a section of the crowd attacked them. The police opened fire. At this, the entire procession attacked the police, and set fire to the police station. Twenty-two policemen were burnt alive. After this incident, Gandhiji decided to withdraw the movement. On February 12, 1922 the Congress Working Committee endorsed his decision and the Non-

16. *Punjab FR, Second Half of April 1921*, F. No. 13, NAI.
17. *Punjab FR, First Half of May 1921*, F. No. 63, NAI.
18. *Punjab FR, First Half of January 1922*, F. No. 18, NAI.
19. *Punjab FR, Second Half of January 1922*, F. No. 18, NAI.
20. *Punjab FR, First Half of February 1922*, F. No. 18, NAI.
21. *Punjab FR, Second Half of July 1922*, F. No. 18, NAI.

Cooperation Movement ended.[22]

On April 6, 1930, the Congress launched another national struggle popularly known as the Civil Disobedience Movement. Gandhiji by picking up a handful of salt at Dandi inaugurated the Civil Disobedience Movement. All over the country the defiance of salt laws started.[23]

In many parts of the country the movement soon took on the form of a no-tax and no-rent campaign. Peasants joined the protest in large numbers. In Andhra Pradesh the movement was soon enmeshed with the campaign against re-settlement that threatened an increase in land revenue. In UP, peasants launched a no-rent campaign. Gandhiji asked them to pay only fifty per cent of the legal rent and get receipts for payment of the full amount. Peasants in Gujarat, mainly in Surat and Kheda, refused to pay their taxes. Their land and movable property were confiscated. In Bihar and Bengal villagers launched a movement against the hated 'chowkidara' tax.[24]

In the Punjab, as a part of the movement, a no-revenue campaign, accompanied by kisan sabhas was launched that demanded a reduction in land revenue and water rates and scaling down the debt.[25] During this movement defiance of salt laws and a campaign to boycott foreign cloth and liquor was started. The attempts were made to sustain a salt 'satyagraha' but the scope for it being limited, concentration soon shifted to the picketing of foreign cloth and liquor shops.[26]

In Haryana people participated in the Civil Disobedience Movement with great enthusiasm. In Rohtak district, the

---

22. Bipan Chandra et al., op.cit., p. 191.
23. Ibid., p. 272.
24. Ibid., pp. 343-344.
25. Ibid., p. 344.
26. Mridula Mukherjee, *Peasants in India's Non-Violent Revolution: Practice and Theory,* New Delhi, 2004, p. 82.

district Congress committee, observed a complete 'hartal' and a public meeting was held.[27] At Ambala, on April 27, 1930, under the leadership of Khan Abdul Gaffar Khan and Pandit Bhagat Ram Sahgal, a procession of satyagrahis was taken out which after passing through the main bazaars and preaching the boycott of foreign cloth and liquor terminated in Anaz Mandi where the salt law was broken by preparing contraband salt. Many women singing national songs also accompanied the procession.[28]

In Rohtak, up to June 17, 1930, thirty-one arrests had been made for instigation of non-payment of land revenue. Out of the total 52 arrests about 30 were peasants belonging to the agriculturist class.[29] The mutiny week (1857) was celebrated here from June 11-16, 1930. Public meetings were held every day in which more than 30,000 people participated including 500 women. On the last day of the week a grand procession paraded the streets of Rohtak. Photos of Rani Laxmi Bai were exhibited.[30]

At the village of Madina in Rohtak, the police was sent to unfurl the national flag which had been hoisted in the village.[31] The government adopted a repressive policy to curb the agitation of the people by prohibiting meetings and processions. However, the movement continued.

Meanwhile, propaganda for boycott of foreign cloth was also being done. Many leaders including Madan Mohan Malviya, Gopi Chand Bhargava, Neki Ram Sharma, Abdul Gaffar Khan and other visited the districts of Haryana to campaign for the boycott of foreign goods.[32] And to a very

27. *The Tribune*, April 10, 1930, and K.C. Yadav, op.cit., p. 68.
28. *The Tribune*, April 29, 1930, p. 7, C. 1.
29. *The Tribune*, June 20, 1930, p. 1, C. 4.
30. Ibid.
31. *Punjab FR, First Half of July 1930*, F. No. 18/7/1930, NAI.
32. Jagdish Chander, 'Political Development in Haryana, 1928-1947', in *Haryana: Studies in History and Politics*, edited by J.N. Singh Yadav, New Delhi, 1976, p. 112.

great extent they achieved their purpose.[33] The traders of all these places agreed not to buy foreign cloth in future. The traders of Rohtak, Bhiwani and Ambala undertook not to import foreign cloth.[34] As a result, the wholesale and retail business of cloth declined.[35]

There were many instances of picketing of liquor shops in Haryana. The main objectives of the picketing were (i) to reduce consumption of liquor and (ii) to curtail the excise revenue. Due to picketing, the consumption of liquor decreased many fold in the Rohtak town.[36]

Non-payment of taxes was also a part of the movement. Some attempts were made to instigate non-payment of taxes in rural areas in the Kaithal tehsil of Karnal district.[37] In the villages of the Skinner Estate near Hansi in the Hissar district, peasants (tenants) had started a non-violent satyagraha movement against the landlords. But soon the movement became a violent agitation. Arrests and prosecutions of peasants (tenants) were launched. The peasants still stood in defiance of the landlords. At last a compromise was reached between the peasants and the landlords.[38] There was also trouble between tenants and landlords at Daulpur in Hissar district and in the village Chhuchhakwas in the Jhajjar tehsil of Rohtak district. Arrests and prosecutions were launched under the general cover of dealing with the Civil Disobedience Movement.[39]

On March 5, 1931, the Gandhi-Irwin Pact was signed and

33. *Punjab FR, First Half of August 1930,* F. No. 18/8/1830, NAI.
34. Jagdish Chander, op.cit., p. 112.
35. *Punjab FR, First Half of August 1930,* F. No. 18/8/1930, NAI.
36. Jagdish Chander, op.cit., p. 112.
37. *Punjab FR First Half of February 1931,* F. No. 18/2/1931, NAI.
38. Jagdish Chander, op.cit., p. 114.
39. Mridula Mukherjee, op.cit., pp. 81-82 and D.C. Office Records, Confidential, F. No. D/3, *Chhuchhkwas Trouble,* 1930, H.S.A. Public Records, Accession No. 8786.

the movement was suspended.[40] Under the pact, political organizations could again begin to function openly and the repressive laws were also repealed.[41] A certain political space which was now available was quickly used by the Congress.[42] In Haryana the Congress agitation was more active and successful particularly in the rural areas.[43] In Rohtak, Hissar and Karnal districts, Congress appointed officials from Deputy Commissioner to 'Thanedar' to set up a parallel government of sorts.[44] At many places the peasants refused to pay land revenue and taxes. Incidents occurred in the villages of Karnal and Kaithal district when Tehsildars, Naib Tehsildars and Qanungos were assaulted while engaged in the collection of land revenue.[45]

The government tried to curb the movement by adopting repressive measures. The Congressmen also reacted strongly. The Civil Disobedience Movement was again started on January 4, 1932. Gandhiji withdrew movement on April 7, 1934.

Many sections of the society including peasants, women and students participated in the movement in Haryana. It had a large impact on the people from the cities as well as on the people from the villages.

After the Civil Disobedience Movement, no major mass struggle occurred till 1940 when the Individual Satyagraha Movement was launched. Political activities were in full swing in Haryana during the Individual Satyagraha Movement. Congress workers like Pandit Sri Ram Sharma, Chaudhri Nanhu Ram, B. Mool Chand Jain, Mr. Dilawar

---

40. K.C. Yadav, *Modern Haryana: History and Culture, 1803-1966*, New Delhi, 2002, p. 180.
41. Mridula Mukherjee, op.cit., p. 93.
42. Ibid.
43. *Punjab FR, Second Half of April 1931*, F. No. 18/4/1931, NAI.
44. See *Punjab FR, between April to June 1931*. NAI.
45. Jagdish Chander, op.cit., p. 118.

Singh and others toured about 30 different villages where they addressed largely attended public meetings. Over a thousand rupees had been collected for the Satyagraha Fund and over 300 Congressmen had signed the Satyagraha pledge in Rohtak.[46] Many Congress workers were arrested in Hissar.[47] Pandit Neki Ram Sharma created a great deal of enthusiasm at Bhiwani in Hissar district by making a patriotic speech and he was sentenced to one and a half years in jail.[48] Pandit Shri Ram Sharma and Lala Shamlal were arrested at Hissar. Chaudhri Sahib Ram was sentenced to nine months' imprisonment and a fine of Rs. 100 for delivering an anti-war speech at Hissar.[49] Nine out of twenty-seven members of the All-India Congress Committee were arrested for civil disobedience, eight were arrested for offences other than formal participation in civil disobedience, eleven out of the twenty-one members of the Provincial Congress Committee were arrested as 'satyagrahis', while six were dealt with for other activities.[50]

This movement continued for fifteen months when it was suspended by Gandhiji. Satyagrahis were released from the jails. The people of Haryana showed great enthusiasm for this movement.

The next round of activity came when Gandhiji launched the Quit India Movement on August 8, 1942. On 9th August the government arrested all the top leaders of the Congress and they were taken to unknown destinations. After this, there was a tremendous mass upsurge all over the country. The people expressed their anger by attacking police stations, post-offices, courts, railway stations and other symbols of government authority. National flags were forcibly hoisted

46. *The Tribune*, January 4, 1941, p. 4, C.2.
47. Ibid., February 5, 1941, p. 4, C.2.
48. *Punjab FR, First Half of December 1940*, F. No. 18/12/1940, NAI.
49. *Punjab FR, First Half of January 1941*, F. No. 18/1/1941, NAI.
50. Ibid.

on public buildings in many places in defiance of the police.[51]

In Haryana there were demonstrations in several districts notably Karnal and Rohtak. Attempts were made to distribute patriotic or anti-government literature and sabotage telephone wires and letter boxes, to tamper with the railway line and to close the schools in the rural areas.[52] There were also two separate attempts to burn down a vernacular record room of the Deputy Commissioner's office at Karnal.[53]

The Congress Party was declared an unlawful organization and its offices, etc. were locked. There were lathi charges and firing for suppressing the movement. In the end the government succeeded in crushing the movement. After this movement there was hardly any political activity in Haryana till the war ended.

In mid 1945 another movement—the pro-Indian National Army (INA) Movement emerged which also became a part of the freedom struggle. During the fighting between the INA and the British Indian Army, about 15,000 INA soldiers were captured.[54] Most of them belonged to the Punjab and Haryana. the British intended to treat the captured INA men as guilty of treason. In the first week of November 1945, the three main INA officers Maj. Gen. Shah Nawaj Khan, Lt. Col. P.K. Sehgal and Lt. Col. G.S. Dhillon were sent to court martial. The Commander-in-Chief decided that the trial should be held in public so that facts revealed by the trial would horrify Indian public opinion.[55]

When these trials began, a new wave of nationalism

---

51. Bipan Chandra et al., *India's Struggle for Independence,* New Delhi, 1989, p. 461.
52. *Punjab FR, Second Half of August 1942,* F. No. 18/8/1942, and *Punjab FR, First Half of September 1942,* 18/9/1942, NAI.
53. *Punjab FR, First Half of October 1942,* F. No. 18/10/1942, NAI.
54. K.K. Ghosh, *Indian National Army,* Meerut, 1969, p. 208.
55. Ibid., p. 203.

spread in Haryana and other parts of the country. Not only people in general but students and political parties and even armed forces showed their sympathy towards the INA officials and personnel. A nation-wide agitation was started against the British policy of punishing the INA officers. During the first trial of INA personnel, a huge crowd gathered outside the Red Fort carrying placards of slogans like "save INA patriots" and "patriots not traitors". The public shouted slogans of Jai Hind as the cars carrying INA officials for the trial passed by.[56]

In Lahore and in many other towns people showed their sympathy for the INA personnel by not holding the usual magnificent Diwali illumination.[57] Students played an important role in demonstrations. They held meetings and paraded in streets, carrying flags and raising slogans "Lal Quila Tor Do, Azad Hind Fauj ko Chhor Do". Punjab University students also held a meeting and adopted a resolution demanding release of INA men and officers.[58]

In Haryana many parts observed complete 'hartal' in sympathy with the INA prisoners. In Rewari, a crowded meeting was held. Rao Gaj Raj Singh of Gurgaon and other local workers addressed the meeting.[59] The INA anti-recruitment propaganda took place in Gurgaon and Ambala districts. Similar activities occurred in the Delhi recruiting area.[60]

People also participated by collecting money for the INA relief fund. The Indian National Army Defence Committee supplied shoes, clothes, medicines, toilet requisites and other

---

56. *The Tribune*, November 6, 1945, p. 1, C.3.
57. Ibid., p. 1, also *Punjab FR, First Half of November 1945*, F. No. 18/11/1945, NAI.
58. Ibid., October 20, 1945, p. 1, C.2.
59. *Hindustan Times*, November 8, 1945, p. 5, C.2.
60. *Home Department, Political, Intelligence Bureau*, F. No. 21/12/1945, NAI.

articles to the members of INA who were detained in Delhi Fort.[61]

The Indian National Congress demanded unconditional release of INA personnel and declared them to be heroes.[62] The Punjab Provincial Congress Committee prepared a memorandum with 80,000 signatures for submission to the Viceroy and Commander-in-Chief.[63]

Other political parties also came forward to support the cause of the INA personnel. The British realized the situation and the Commander-in-Chief remitted the sentence of transportation passed by court martial against the INA officers and they were set free.[64]

Thus, it is evident that the people of Haryana region, including the peasants, participated in different struggles and waves of the National Movement. It is clear that the people of Haryana provided support and allegiance to the national cause.

II

Acts of protest, revolts, or movements are mostly a product of a consciousness of rights being threatened or new rights being desired. They also reflect the protestors' understanding of their social, economic and political condition. The peasants of Haryana were aware that their economic and social condition was not good in the early 20th century. Socially they were backward.[65] In the caste hierarchy the peasants or agriculturalist caste were categorized in the middle or lower level. They were called 'zamindars' but they were mostly

---

61. *The Tribune*, November 6, 1945, p. 9, C.1.
62. *Transfer of Power (1942-47)*, Vol. VI, New Delhi 1976, pp. 305-306.
63. *The Tribune*, November 3, 1945, p. 1, C.4.
64. N.N. Mitra, *Indian Annual Register*, 1946, Vol. 1, p. 298 and *The Tribune*, January 4, 1946, p. 1, C.1.
65. See Chapter 1.

peasant proprietors and carried on the work of agriculture by means of family labour. Most of these were in debt and their land was mortgaged to the moneylenders.[66] The burden of land revenue was also heavy.

That peasants were becoming conscious of their interests, is shown by the way Chaudhri Chhotu Ram describes them. About the peasants he said, "He (the lion) lay fast asleep for ages in the forest of economics, and the economic jackal and foxes nibbled at him and tugged at his tail and mane. But now he is showing definite signs of waking up".[67]

As we have shown above, the Indian National Movement led by the Indian National Congress played an important role in spreading nationalist consciousness among the peasants. In the elections also the political parties were very active in this matter. Peasants participated in the nationalist movement which was anti-imperialist in nature.[68]

Communal ideology also affected the consciousness of the people. In the elections, because the electorates were divided on communal lines the leaders tried to spread communal consciousness among the peasantry. Their success was fairly limited till the mid–1940s. During the partition the communal consciousness had reached the level of communal violence which was the result of the communal propaganda by political parties and other communal groups.[69]

National consciousness also existed among the peasantry. They were aware of the colonial exploitation by imperial rule. The land revenue and other taxes were fixed at a very high rate and extracted by the government. Therefore the peasants wanted redressal of their economic

---

66. See Chapter 1.
67. *Punjab Legislative Assembly Debate (PLAD)*, November 16, 1938, Vol.VI, No. 6. Lahore, 1939, p. 357, NMML.
68. See Chapter 3, Part 1.
69. See Chapter 2.

grievances. Other forms of consciousness that existed among the peasants were caste consciousness and regional consciousness.

III

During the colonial period, nationalism was the only ideology which expressed the experience of the colonized people of cultural marginalization, economic exploitation and the political subordination.[70]

The Nationalist Movement during the Gandhian phase acquired a mass base because of the peasants' participation in it. Influenced by nationalist ideology, the peasants participated in the movements of Non-Cooperation, Civil Disobedience and the Quit India Movement.

In Haryana during the elections of 1937 the majority of peasants supported the Unionists because they believed that this party would solve their economic problems. During these elections, the Congress Party failed to get support of the peasants.[71] It does not mean that the peasants had no nationalist ideology or the ideology based on nationalism. It is clear that the Unionist Party was a provincial party but the Congress was a national party. The main issue for the Congress Party was the freedom of the country.

There is no doubt that peasants wanted to redress their economic grievances. The peasants supported the Unionist Party because this party considered the peasants' issue as the main issue. However in the elections of 1946 the peasants supported the Congress Party in Haryana because the party successfully approached the peasants and they thought that Congress was the only party which gave them freedom from the colonial exploitation as well.

Peasants joined the British army because the profession of agriculture was not sufficient for their survival. They

70. Mridula Mukherjee, op.cit., p. 318.
71. See Chapter 2.

joined the British army not to support the British rule but for their livelihood. It does not mean that the peasants did not have the ideology of nationalism. They joined the British army because of 'bhuq' (hunger).[72]

Peasants joined the British army to fight with poverty and starvation and to fight with the famines which occurred at least once or twice in a generation.[73] Therefore, they joined the British army due to economic necessity to avoid starvation during the time of famine. They regarded enlistment as a "safety-net".[74] But during the Second World War the Indian soldiers of the INA fought the British army. This was actually due to the ideology of nationalism and they gave the slogan of 'Jai Hind'.

In Haryana there were two major political parties at that time – the Unionist and the Congress. If we talk about the ideology of these political parties the Unionist ideology was pro-agriculturist and pro-rural while the Congress at that time was popular among urban people and was trying to spread their influence to the countryside. The Unionists wanted to stop the economic exploitation of peasants by the moneylenders while the Congress wanted to stop the colonial exploitation. Unionists also talked about the domination of urban people on the rural in different fields like government jobs and education. The Unionists favoured the peasantry and the rural people.

On the other hand, Congress Party in Haryana attached itself with the issue of freedom. Their primary concern was to win freedom and after that solve the social and economic issues. In other states where the Congress Party assumed

72. M.L. Darling, *Rusticus Loquitur, or the Old Light and the New in the Punjab Villages*, London, 1930, p. 30.
73. Tan Tai Yong, *The Garrison State: The Military, Government and Society in Colonial Punjab, 1849-1947*, New Delhi, 2005, p. 79.
74. Ibid., p. 84.

office in 1937 was responsible for rent and revenue reductions.[75]

Till 1946, in Haryana the communal ideology propagated by the communal parties was not successful in the countryside or among the peasantry. The anti-imperialist ideology was the main ideology of the peasantry during the nationalist movement in Haryana. This ideology united the peasantry which was divided on the basis of caste, religion and language.[76]

IV

The political mobilization on an extensive scale of the peasants in Haryana and on all-India basis began during the freedom struggle, particularly by the early 20th century when the British introduced the franchise system. The various political parties such as Unionists Party, Congress Party and other political parties in Haryana tried to mobilize the peasants in different ways.

The Punjab National Unionist Party which formed in 1923 was predominantly rural-oriented.[77] It mobilized the peasants reinforcing their rural orientation while demarcating it distinctively and antagonistically from the urban sector.[78] Under the new provincial autonomy scheme in 1937 efforts were made to improve the rural and peasants' condition. Unionists made rural-oriented legislations and mobilized the rural people.[79]

---

75. Mridula Mukherjee, op.cit., p. 350.
76. Ibid., p. 322.
77. Madan Gopal, *Sir Chhotu Ram: The Man and the Vision*, Ghaziabad, 1997, p. 54.
78. Paul Wallace, 'Peasant Mobilization in India and the Contemporary Political Significance of Sir Chhotu Ram', in *Indian Journal of Political Science*, Vol. 41, No. 1, March 1980, p. 686.
79. Ibid.

In Haryana the peasants were economically and socially backward. The Unionists mobilized the rural people around the ideology of pro-peasants and pro-rural. According to them villagers or peasants were backward and less educated compared to the urban people. They used the rural grievances against the domination of urban people and the exploitation of peasants by the moneylenders.[80] Under their government in the Punjab the Unionists mobilized the peasants by giving a popular slogan "Raj Karega Jat" made in a public meeting at Rohtak in 1944,[81] which means the peasant shall rule.

The Unionists also mobilized the peasants by their writings in newspapers. Chaudhri Chhotu Ram wrote many articles on the condition of the peasants in *Jat Gazette*. By these articles he mobilized the peasants against their exploitation by moneylenders, the merchants and the bureaucrats.[82] He also tried to unite the peasants which were divided on caste and communal lines. He advised the peasantry to fight for their rights. He exhorted them to raise their voice instead of remaining silent.

Some Unionists also played leading roles in the enlistment during the war (First World War). By their efforts they got official patronage. Chaudhri Chhotu Ram was given considerable political influence within the peasant community in Haryana.[83] He mobilized the peasants to join the British army in order to remove their unemployment, poverty and to improve their economic condition. By this the peasants benefited and these leaders got government patronage as well as they became popular among the peasantry.

---

80. See Chapter 1 and 2.
81. Prem Chowdhry, *Punjab Politics: The Role of Sir Chhotu Ram*, New Delhi, 1984. p. 54.
82. Madan Gopal, op.cit., pp. 65-67.
83. Tan Tai Yong, op.cit., p. 132.

In the wake of the nationalist movement the peasants became politicized.[84] The Indian National Movement organized the peasantry and led their struggles. Political workers and cadres activated by the national movement were to form the cadre of peasants' movement as well.[85]

The Non-Cooperation Movement, Civil Disobedience Movement and Quit India Movement played an important role to mobilize the peasants against the colonial rule not only in Haryana but also other parts of the country. It developed the anti-imperialist ideology based on the full-fledged critique of colonialism and especially its ramifications on the peasants and agricultural under-development.[86]

Mahatma Gandhi evolved the techniques of peasants' mobilization including meetings, processions, signature campaign, and satyagraha which corresponded to the agrarian programme of the Congress that included reduction of rent and revenue, abolition of feudal dues and levies, fixity of tenure and moratorium of debts.[87]

The Indian National Movement started the mobilization of peasants in the Gandhian phase. "An entirely new dynamic and political revolutionary tendency has come to be imported into the peasants' struggle by Mahatma Gandhi".[88] He led the peasants struggle against the indigo planters and land revenue system in Champaran in Bihar and Kaira in Gujarat respectively.

The pattern of Gandhiji's mobilization of peasants was also adopted in Haryana by the Congress members. They

84. Sunil Sen, *Peasants Movement in India: Mid-Nineteenth and Twentieth Century*, New Delhi, 1982, p. 28.
85. Mridula Mukherjee, op.cit., p. 314.
86. Satya M.Rai, *Legislative Politics and the Freedom Struggle in the Punjab, 1897-1947*, New Delhi, 1984, see Preface (xiv).
87. Sunil Sen, op.cit., p. 29.
88. N.G. Ranga, *Revolutionary Peasants*, New Delhi, 1949, p. 41.

mobilized the peasants at the tehsil, district and provincial level. They not only organized the peasantry on class lines but also of national freedom. In the Gandhian phase, influenced by the nationalist ideology, peasants participated in the nationalist movement on a large scale due to which it became a mass movement.

4

On the Road to Empowerment

The British introduced a new legal system, new tenurial system, collection of land revenue in cash and intensified the commercialization of agriculture. The peasants had to take loans from the moneylenders to pay the land revenue in cash and for other expenses. Therefore the importance of the moneylenders increased tremendously. The new legal system also gave the moneylenders rights over the peasants' produce and land which they never had earlier. These changes created a situation due to which the indebtedness of the peasants and the transfer of their land to the moneylenders had become the main feature of the agrarian economy.[1]

In several provinces there occurred or threatened to occur serious agrarian unrest due to the loss of land by the hereditary landholding classes.[2] The government adopted various measures to meet this political threat. A series of legislations were made by the government. The most important was the enactment in 1900 of the Punjab Alienation of Land Act which prohibited the transfer of land from the agriculturist tribes to the non-agriculturist tribes.[3]

---

1. See Chapter 1.
2. Norman G. Barrier, 'The Formulation of Enactment of the Punjab Alienation of Land Bill', *The Punjab Past and Present*, Vol. XIII-I, April 1979, Serial No. 25, p. 193.
3. The Punjab Alienation of Land Act, 1900 [Act No. XIII of 1900], *The Punjab Code*, Vol. 1, Lahore 1937, p. 830.

According to the Act, the permanent alienation of land was only possible if "the alienor is a member of a agricultural tribe and the alienee is a member of the same tribe or of a tribe in the same group."[4] But the non-agriculturists were at liberty permanently to alienate land through sales, exchange, gifts and wills.[5]

Curzon supported the Bill and emphasized that most Punjab officials favoured the legislation. Initially the Congress was against the Bill. The Congress resolution of 1899 attacking the legislation underlined the dangers of tampering with natural credit relations and warned that the Punjab land market would be ruined. But the Congress was unable to take a firm stand against the alienation bill and its next session at Lahore the Congress dropped the alienation discussion from the agenda.[6]

The result of this Act was that moneylenders, shopkeepers, and professional men belonging to 'non-agriculturist' castes and tribes could not buy land from hereditary cultivators, or hold such land on mortgage for more than twenty years, without the consent of the state. An important provision was that the land of a hereditary cultivator could not be sold in execution of a decree.[7]

However, while some peasants possibly benefited from this Act but the problem of indebtedness continued. The peasants fell deeper and deeper into debt. By 1929, the total debt in the Punjab province was over 330 crores. This meant that if the debt was evenly distributed among the population, each person would owe more than one year's income to the moneylender.[8] Moneylending to agriculturists had become

4. Ibid.
5. Ibid.
6. Norman G. Barrier, op.cit., pp. 208-210.
7. M.S. Randhawa, *A History of Agriculture in India*, Vol. III, 1757-1947, New Delhi, 1983, p. 278.
8. Norman G. Barrier, op.cit., pp. 214-215.

the Punjab's largest industry.[9]

According to a rural indebtedness committee report of 1933 the agricultural debt was 135 crores, twelve times the revenue of the province. Even the interest thereon would amount to double the provincial income. As per the recommendations, ancestral land could be attached even after the death of the debtor.[10]

A demand arose to protect the peasants from the moneylenders. In the Punjab Legislative Council, Chaudhri Chhotu Ram said:

> The debtor classes form as high a proportion as 90 per cent of the population of the whole province. The whole economic fabric of the province depends on the prosperity of these classes. If these classes perish, economically, I think every other section of the population will have ultimately to perish. Therefore it is really no act of obligation to the debtor classes that they should be kept alive and healthy.[11]

A member of the rural indebtedness committee warned the government:

> If you persist in such a course and the indebted peasants who are sinking lower and lower, find that the governments are impotent to protect them from sahukars, the time will soon come when they will protect themselves, with their own hands.[12]

There was also some evidence of growing resentment against moneylenders among the peasantry. There were reports that murders of moneylenders by their debtors were increasing

---

9. M.L. Darling, *The Punjab Peasant in Prosperity and Debt*, New Delhi, 1978.
10. N.N. Mitra (ed.), *The Indian Annual Register (1919-1947)*, 1933, Vol.1, New Delhi, 1990, p. 230.
11. *Punjab Legislative Council Debates*, November 21, 1935, Vol. XXVII, p. 1017.
12. N.N. Mitra (ed.), op. cit., p. 230.

everyday.[13]

The government realized the situation and took steps by making Acts to give relief to the indebted peasants. These Acts were the Punjab Relief of Indebtedness Act, 1934 and the Punjab Debtors' Protection Act, 1936.[14]

The Punjab Relief of Indebtedness Act of 1934 controlled the rate of interest chargeable by the moneylenders. The Act adopted the principle of Damdupat. According to this principle no court could grant a decree in satisfaction of both the principal and interest for a larger sum than twice the amount which the court found had been due at the commencement of the Act by the debtors.[15] This was done through the Debt Conciliation Boards. This also barred the jurisdiction of Civil Courts and the debtors were exempted from arrest under this law.[16]

The Punjab Debtors Protection Act, 1936 sought to provide greater protection to the debtors by giving the exemption of ancestral property from liability. In other words it exempted the temporary alienation of the ancestral property in execution of a decree of loan incurred by any predecessor in interest. The standing crops, other than sugarcane, cotton and trees were exempted from attachment and sale. This Act also had a provision:

> Whenever civil court orders that land be attached and alienated temporarily in the execution of a decree for the payment of money the proceedings of such attachment and alienation shall be transferred to the collector and the collector shall decide the period of alienation which shall not exceed twenty years

---

13. Prem Chowdhry, *Punjab Politics: The Role of Sir Chhotu Ram*, New Delhi, 1984, p. 252.
14. The Punjab Relief of Indebtedness Act, 1934 (Punjab Act No. VII of 1934), *The Punjab Code*, Vol. II, Lahore, 1937, pp. 739-754.
15. Ibid., p. 752.
16. Ibid., pp. 739-754.

> in the case of land owned by a member of a statutory agricultural tribe. And the collector had power to exempt any portion of land from alienation if it is necessitated for the subsistence of the debtor.[17]

After their success in the elections of 1937 and the formation of provincial government, the Unionist Party passed a series of legislations in 1938. The main Acts were:[18]

I. Punjab Alienation of Land (Amendment) Act, (April 11, 1938). To prohibit agricultural land being put to destructive use by a mortgagee or lessee without the consent of the owner, and to remove ambiguity regarding the period for which temporary alienation of land belonging to a statutory agriculturist judgement debtor can be ordered by a civil court.

II. Punjab Debtors' Protection (Amendment) Bill (June 21, 1938). To prohibit execution of civil decrees by the appointment of a receiver to administer property which is protected from attachment or sale under the colonization of Government Land (Punjab) Act, 1912.

III. Punjab Registration of Moneylenders Act (July 16, 1938). To establish effective control on the business of moneylending by compelling moneylenders to obtain licenses.

IV. Punjab Alienation of Land (Second Amendment) Bill (July 16, 1938). To nullify certain sales and mortgages of land which were effected in contravention of the intention of the Punjab Alienation of Land Act of 1900.

---

17. The Punjab Debtors' Protection Act, 1936 (Punjab Act No. II of 1936), *The Punjab Code*, Vol. II, Lahore, 1937, pp. 789-795.
18. N.N. Mitra (ed.), *The Indian Annual Register*, Vol. II, July-December 1938, p. 202.

V. Punjab Restitution of Mortgaged Lands Act (July 21, 1938). To terminate old mortgages of land (effected before 1901 and still subsisting) on payment of a reasonable compensation where necessary by the mortgager to the mortgagee.

VI. Punjab Alienation of Land (Third Amendment) Act (July 22, 1938). To place the agriculturist moneylender for the purposes of the Punjab Alienation of Land Act, in the same position as non-agriculturist moneylenders and check them from permanently acquiring the land of their agriculturist debtors.

These bills were called the "Golden Bills" by the Unionist while the opposition called them the "Black Bills".[19] In the legislative assembly there were heated debates when these Bills were introduced. When the Punjab Debtors Protection (Amendment) Bill was introduced in the Assembly, a member, Khan Bahadur Chaudhri Riasat Ali, from a rural constituency, said in support of the Bill:

> We forget the famous words of Mr. Calvert that "credit holds the borrower as a rope holds a hanged man". This credit is the most dangerous thing going about the financial world.[20]

The Punjab Registration of Moneylenders Act, 1938 provided for the elimination of malpractices by establishing control on the business of moneylending by compelling the moneylenders to obtain licences.[21] The licence could be

19. *Punjab Legislative Assembly Debates (PLAD)* (1937-1946). NMML.
20. *PLAD*, April 5, 1938, Vol. IV, No. 10, Official Report, Lahore, 1938, p. 701, NMML.
21. M.S. Randhawa, op.cit., p. 364; Satya M. Rai, *Legislative Politics and Freedom Struggle in the Punjab, 1897-1947*, New Delhi, 1984, pp. 248-249; Prem Chowdhry, 'Rural Relations Prevailing in the Punjab at the Time of Enactment of the So-called 'Golden Laws' or Agrarian Legislation of the Late Thirties', *The Punjab Past and Present*, Vol. X-II, October 1976, p. 479.

suspended by the collector for a fixed period, if the moneylender was found guilty of an offence by a law court. In the absence of a licence, or during its suspension, the moneylender was disqualified from recovering his loan. This Bill was to be applicable to all moneylenders including the agriculturist moneylenders who had taken the money-lending as a principal or subsidiary business.[22]

While supporting the Bill the Premier Sir Sikandar Hyat Khan said:

> It is very likely that this legislation instead of doing moneylenders damage will do them good. I am quite certain that it will have that effect. It will mean that dishonest moneylenders will go away and honest moneylenders will flourish.[23]

The Unionist Ministry also made three amendments to the Punjab Alienation of Land Act in 1938. The first amendment prohibited agricultural land being put to destructive use by a mortgagee or a lessee, without the consent of the owner and removed the ambiguity regarding the period for which temporary alienation of land belonging to the statutory agriculturist debtor could be ordered by a civil court.[24]

The second amendment declared invalid all 'benami' transactions of lands made in contravention of the Land Alienation Act, 1901. The Punjab Alienation of Land Act, 1901, had prohibited the members of the agriculturist tribes from alienating their land permanently in favour of the non-agriculturists. But the land was nominally transferred by one agriculturist to another, but the buyer whose name appeared in the official records was only a dummy under whose cover the 'non-agriculturist' enjoyed the actual possession of the

22. *PLAD*, 1938, Vol. V, pp. 978-89, cited in Satya M. Rai, op.cit., pp. 248-249.
23. Ibid., June 24, 1938, Vol. V, No. 4, Lahore, 1938, p. 252.
24. Madan Gopal, *Sir Chhotu Ram: A Political Biography*, Delhi, 1977, p. 107.

land and its income. The total value of such 'benami' mortgages in the Punjab Province was estimated at Rs. 150 to 160 million.[25]

There was a criticism about the Punjab Alienation of Land Act (Amendments I and II) that it only checks the exploitation of one section of moneylenders, i.e. non-agriculturist moneylenders. The critics argued that it did not cover the agriculturist moneylenders.[26] For this, the Unionist government made a third amendment (July 22, 1938) in this Act by which agriculturist moneylenders were placed in the same position as non-agriculturist moneylenders and checked them from permanently acquiring the land of their agriculturist debtors.[27]

While supporting these bills, the Premier Sir Sikander Hyat Khan, said:

> The moneylender is an institution, a necessary institution and a very beneficial institution and this institution has been in existence not since the advent of the British Raj or during the last century but from times immemorial and the moneylender is a part and parcel of the village community. But then he was respected, loved and held in esteem by the village community. Why, because there was a moral sanction and the sanction of the panchayat in the village society and social sanction behind him, but when the British bureaucracy came here, what happened? They enacted laws which gave undue shelter as laissez faire to these people and they converted the honest moneylenders into the dishonest moneylenders. I am inclined to blame the British bureaucracy for most of the troubles which the agriculturist is suffering at the hands of moneylenders, for turning an honest moneylender into a dishonest moneylender

---

25. M.S. Randhawa, op.cit., p. 365.
26. Article by A.K. Ghosh, 'Deepening Crises in Punjab', *The National Front*, July 3, 1938, cited in *Towards Freedom*, op.cit., p. 2585.
27. N.N. Mitra (ed.), *The Indian Annual Register*, Vol. II, July-December 1938, p. 202.

> by passing anti-usury legislation and it is for that reason that we have to bring forward measures to undo the mischief that was done during that period when undue shelter was given to such people. That is our unfortunate and unpleasant duty. But let me assure you that this government in spite of the chaffing and in spite of the accusations will stand firm like a rock and will see that dishonest moneylenders are again converted into honest moneylenders as they used to be.[28]

The Restitution of Mortgaged Lands Act, 1938 was also introduced in the same session which terminated old mortgages of land (affected before 1901) on payment of a reasonable compensation when necessary by the mortgagor to the mortgagee. This act enabled 306,738 mortgagors to redeem 756,131 acres of mortgaged land.[29]

Another important legislation the Punjab Agricultural Produce Markets Acts, 1939 was passed by the Unionist Government to secure a fair price for agriculturists' produce. By this Act the government established market committees. This Act was popularly called the Mandi Act.[30]

When this Bill was introduced in the Assembly, Chaudhri Chhotu Ram said:

> When he (peasant) reaps his crop he is the owner of his produce, but when he brings his produce into the neighbouring market he ceases to be the owner of his produce. The brokers, weighmen, measurers, and several other persons all combine to exploit this village simpleton.

He further said that "something must be done to save the poor peasants from the clutches of the clever market people".[31]

---

28. *PLAD*, June 21, 1938, Vol.V, No. 2, Official Report, p. 137, NMML.
29. Satya M. Rai, op.cit., pp. 250-251.
30. Pardaman Singh, *Chhotu Ram in the Eyes of His Contemporaries*, New Delhi, 1992, p.28.
31. *PLAD*, July 7, 1938, Vol. V. pp. 804-805.

According to the Punjab Banking Enquiry Report, on an average, as many as 41 weights out of 100 were to be found false and 69 per cent of the scales tested were found to be incorrect. Further, some of the shopkeepers were found to be keeping two sets of weights, one for buying and other for selling.[32]

Dr. Gopi Chand Bhargava also realized this and in a meeting held at Sonepat he said that "the prices of agricultural commodities should be improved and brought under control because the innocent agriculturists are not generally offered the right prices in the markets."[33]

This Bill was aimed at protecting the growers of agricultural commodities from various malpractices of shopkeepers and brokers.[34] One of these provisions was that two-third representation was given to the peasants in the market committees.[35]

The main features of this Act were:[36]

(1) The government control over the purchase and sale of agriculturist produce was established. Only the licence holder carried on purchase and sale of agricultural produce in the specified area.

(2) Establishment of market committees with certain powers and duties. Two-third seats were reserved for growers in market committees.

(3) The duty of market committees included issuing of licences to brokers, weighmen, measurers, surveyors and warehousemen for carrying on their occupation in that market area.

---

32. Ibid., p. 805.
33. Ibid., p. 812.
34. Satya M. Rai, op.cit., p. 251.
35. Madan Gopal, op.cit., p. 107.
36. *The Punjab Government Gazette (Extraordinary),* May 1, 1939, pp. 105-111, also *The Punjab Code,* Vol. II, 7th edition, Simla, 1953, pp. 888-910.

(4) Market committees had the power to levy fees on the agricultural produce bought and sold by licensees in the notified area.

(5) All money received by a market committee was diverted to the market committee fund.

(6) The market committee fund was to be used for the following purposes:

(a) The acquisition of a site or sites for the market.
(b) The maintenance and improvement of the market.
(c) The construction and repair of buildings which were necessary for the purposes of such a market and for the health, convenience and the safety of the persons using it.
(d) The provision and maintenance of standard weights and measures.
(e) The pay, leave allowances, gratuities, compassionate allowances and contribution towards leave allowances or provident fund of the persons employed by the market committee.
(f) The payment of interest on loans that may be raised for purposes of the market and the provision of a sinking fund in respect of such loans.
(g) The collection and dissemination of information regarding all matters relating to crop statistics and marketing in respect of the agricultural produce concerned and propaganda in favour of agricultural improvement and thrift.
(h) Providing comforts and facilities, such as shelter, shade, parking accommodation and water for the persons, draught cattle and pack animals coming to the market, and similar other purposes.
(i) The expenses incurred in auditing the accounts of the committee.
(j) With the previous sanction of the government, any other purposes which were calculated to promote the general interest of the market and

(k) For the payment of travelling allowance to the members of the market committee.

When the Bill was introduced, and certain vested interests raised a hue and cry in the Assembly. Chaudhri Chhotu Ram remarked:

> It is very curious to note that whenever any legislation calculated to protect agriculturalists against their exploitation by capitalists is introduced in this House an un-becoming hue and cry is raised against it.[37]

Chaudhri Chhotu Ram further said:

> Live and let live is the keynote of our policy. None should suffer and none should try to swallow others. Show a little fairness to the exploited zamindars (peasant proprietors) of this province, and we will not give you any cause of anxiety. It will also save you the constant trouble of interrupting my speech. Fairness and patience will be the panacea for almost all your ills. But at present you are in an abnormal mood. You get infuriated at even the slightest hint that it will make to the evils of capitalism.[38]

Dr. Sir Gokul Chand Narang, the leader of the Punjab Provincial Hindu Sabha, opposed the Bills and estimated the peasants' worth about "two penny half penny" and worried about how a peasant could sit alongside a millionaire trader in the market committee.[39]

Chaudhri Chhotu Ram in his reply to Gokul Chand Narang said, "He (peasant) is not a half penny, two penny nonentity, but a proud feeder of all. He gives you food to eat and clothes to wear". He continued, "now this 'lord of the plough' is also the lord of the province whom every millionaire willy-nilly pays, and shall continue to pay

---

37. *PLAD*, November 16, 1938, Vol. VI, No. 6, Lahore 1939, p. 358, NMML.
38. *PLAD*, 1938, Vol. VI, p. 356.
39. Ibid, p. 238.

homage". He also said that sitting side by side with a peasant in a committee is not humiliating, but a source of honour to a landless businessman, though a millionaire.[40]

This act was strongly opposed by the traders and 'hartals' were observed in various parts of the Punjab province. And it delayed the implementation of this Act by nearly two years.[41]

In the Punjab, the Congress members were in a dilemma whether they should support the agrarian legislations or not. They could not oppose the agrarian legislation because these were aimed at giving relief to the indebted peasantry. Dr. Gopi Chand Bhargava, the leader of the Punjab Congress Party, wrote about the Land Alienation (Amendment) Bill:

> I do not oppose it but I cannot support it either. The party has decided to remain non-voting. Now they want to vote for the Bill. They are going into some lobby with government and thus show to the masses that they are the protectors of rights of the masses. I am in agreement that relief is to be given to the poor but I do not support such expropriation.[42]

Lala Duni Chand, a member of the Congress Party in the Punjab Legislative Assembly from the Ambala rural constituency, came out in support of the Registration of Moneylenders Bill:

> Our position as stated in the manifesto is that we want wholeheartedly to ameliorate the financial and economic condition of the peasantry by adopting every possible means. The Congress would wish to raise the level of the economic life of the peasantry and the labourer even before the sun sets today

---

40. Ibid., p. 356.
41. Pardaman Singh, op.cit., p. 28.
42. Gopichand Bhargava to Maulana Azad, July 16, 1938, in Valmiki Chaudhary (ed.), *Dr. Rajendra Prasad Correspondence*, Vol. 2, pp. 188-90 cited in *Towards Freedom: Documents on the Movement for Independence in India*, 1938, Part-3, edited by Basudev Chatterji, New Delhi, 1999, p. 2589.

> so that every one of them could have sufficient food, clothing and housing.[43]

He further said:

> I want to assure the government on behalf of my party that we are at one with the government in extending every protection to the debtors against the abuses and wrong doings of the moneylenders. I even concede that some evil-minded moneylenders exploit simple-minded debtors and in some cases accounts are tampered with. If the intention of the government is really to help the debtors we are prepared to help them in every difficulty the government may have to face.[44]

Mostly Congress members in the Punjab Assembly came from the urban constituencies and represented the urban interests and they remained neutral on this issue. But the members from the rural constituencies voted for the Bills. The Congress was divided on the issue.[45]

The Punjab Governor Sir Henry Craik described the Punjab Congress Party's position in the assembly accurately. He said:

> The Congress Party in the Assembly has, on the other hand, been placed in a difficult position. Most of the Congress members represent urban constituencies, where trading and moenylending interests are strong, and in their hearts they are strongly opposed to the Bills, which are unquestionably prejudicial to the interest of the moneylending classes. They have, however, received stringent orders from the Congress High Command that they are not to oppose the Bills, and the result has been that the majority of the Congress members have remained neutral on all divisions, while the comparatively few Congress members who represent rural constituencies have voted for the Bills.[46]

---

43. *PLAD*, 1938, Vol. V, p. 997.
44. Ibid., p. 998.
45. Mridula Mukherjee, *Peasants in India's Non-Violent Resolution: Practice and Theory*, New Delhi, 2004, p. 167.
46. Letter, H.D. Craik to Brabourne, July 8, 1938, compiled in *Towards Freedom*, op.cit., p. 2586.

The Congress High Command was in favour the Bills. It believed that these measures were designed to give relief to the peasantry. Maulana Abul Kalam Azad gave instructions to Dr. Gopi Chand Bhargava, the leader of the Congress Party in the Assembly to vote for the Bills.[47] Gopi Chand Bhargava received the following telegram from Abul Kalam Azad:

> Hope you have decided to vote for the Bills according to my instructions.

To this he sent the following reply:

> Your orders will be obeyed. Permit me to resign from the Assembly. Cannot lead the party.[48]

In this way, the Congress High Command was in support of the Bills and even Dr. Gopi Chand Bhargava's personal opinion was that these Acts gave relief to the poor. Pandit Sri Ram Sharma, member of the Congress Party in the Legislative Assembly, who officially represented south-eastern towns but who had a solid peasant base in the Rohtak area voted for the Bills.[49] Therefore, the Congress High Command was in favour of the Bills while the Punjab Congress Party was divided on this issue and it was unable to take a stand and at the end remained neutral.

The popularity of the Bills as well as the Unionist Party was increased among the peasants. The Punjab Governor H.D. Craik noted that:

> There can be no doubt that the prestige of the Ministry and its supporters has been greatly increased by the passage of the agrarian legislation. In the two districts I have visited during

47. Letter, H.D. Craik to Brabourne, July 22, 1938, edited in *Towards Freedom* 1938, op.cit., p. 2590.
48. Letter, Craik to Borabourne, July 22, 1938, published in *Punjab Politics, 1936-39: The Start of Provincial Autonomy – Governor's Fortnightly Reports and other Key Documents,* compiled and edited by Lionel Carter, New Delhi, 2004, p. 240.
49. Mridula Mukherjee, op.cit., p. 167.

> the course of my present tour, Ambala and Karnal, I have found that a great majority of my visitors, and all who are either owners or cultivators of land, are enthusiastic in their support of the Bills, and there is no doubt that they command the approval of the majority.[50]

He continued: "There seems to be a widespread impression that the tillers of the soil are now beginning to get a square deal."[51] He further argued about the Acts that "its passage from the Punjab economic point of view is to be welcomed."[52]

These Acts were very popular among the peasantry. According to a Punjab Fortnightly Report:

> The popularity of the Bills among all classes of agriculturists has been strikingly illustrated by the enthusiasm of the many thousands of peasants who assembled to welcome and listen to the speeches of the Hon'ble Minister of Development (Chaudhri Chhotu Ram) during his recent tour of districts in the South-West and Central Punjab.[53]

Sir Sikandar Hyat Khan, the Premier and his colleagues visited twelve districts and addressed public meetings which lasted a little more than three weeks.[54] Chaudhri Chhotu Ram arranged a public meeting at Sonipat. It was attended by one lakh peasants.[55] This shows that there was a mass following behind these demands.

Other conferences followed at Lyallpur and Gujrat in the Punjab. These were equally well attended. The conference

---

50. Letter, Craik to Brabourne, August 24, 1938, Linlithgow papers, published in *Punjab Politics, 1936-1939: The Start of Provincial Autonomy—Governors' Fortnightly Reports and Other Key Documents*, compiled and edited by Lionel Carter, New Delhi, 2004, p. 246.
51. Ibid.
52. Ibid., p. 247.
53. *Punjab FR, First Half of August 1938*, F. No. 18/8/1938, NAI.
54. *Punjab FR, Second Half of October 1938*, F. No. 18/10/1938, NAI.
55. M.S. Randhawa, op.cit., p. 365.

held at Lyallpur by the Unionist Party on September 3rd and 4th was also an unqualified success.[56]

Other Acts and amendments were made by the provincial government to help the agriculturists. These were:[57]

(i) The Punjab Debtors Protection (Amendment) Act IX of 1938.
(ii) The Punjab Debtors Protection (Amendment) Act X of 1939.
(iii) The Punjab Relief of Indebtedness (Amendment) Act XII of 1940.
(iv) The Punjab Agricultural Produce Markets (Amendment) Act IX of 1941.
(v) The Punjab Weights and Measures Act XII of 1941.
(vi) The Punjab Sugarcane (Amendment) Act IX of 1943.
(vii) The Punjab Agricultural Produce Markets (Amendments) Act X of 1944, etc.

These amendments were made to remove the loopholes in these Acts. The Punjab Relief of Indebtedness Act of 1934 was amended in 1940. The main features of this Act were:[58]

(1) Establishment of one Conciliation Board in every district to reduce the debt amount amicably, of which some part was to be paid immediately and the rest in instalments. These Boards could

---

56. *Punjab FR, First Half of September 1938*, F. No. 18/9/1938. NAI.
57. See, *the Punjab Government Gazette, Extraordinary*, 1938-44 also *The Punjab Code*, Vol. II, 7th edition, Simla, 1953.
58. The Punjab Relief of Indebtedness Act, 1934 (Punjab Act No. VII of 1934), *The Punjab Code*, Vol. II, Lahore 1937, pp. 189-195 also the Punjab Relief of Indebtedness Act, 1934 (Punjab Act No. VII of 1934) (As modified up to October 5, 1940), Lahore 1941, pp. 1-22, also *The Punjab Code*, Vol. II, 7th edition, Simla, 1953, pp. 781-803, also cited in Anil Kumar Rathee and D.S. Nandal, *Sir Chhotu Ram and Punjab Economy Under Imperialism*, Rohtak, 1997, pp. 174-175.

conciliate in cases involving debts not exceeding Rs. 10,000.

(2) The maximum rate of interest was lowered to 12 per cent per annum simple interest or 9 per cent per annum with compound interest with yearly rests on secured loans while on unsecured loans it was fixed at 18 ¾ per cent per annum simple interest or 14 per cent compound interest with half yearly rests.

(3) In no case was the interest amount to be allowed in excess of the principal loaned after 1934. But the Imperial Bank or any banking company registered before 1937 under the Indian Companies Act (1913) and the cooperative societies were exempted from the purview of this clause. Banking companies registered since 1937 were not given this exemption because some moneylenders, after the passage of this Act, had organized themselves into banks to realize their old debts.

(4) Houses and other dwellings and sites *appurtenant thereto* could not be attached or sold unless they were proved to have been lying vacant for more than a year.

(5) The temporary alienation of the land belonging to the judgement debtor was also not allowed.

(6) The debtor against whom a decree had been issued could not be arrested for the non-payment of the debt.

(7) The word agriculturist included agricultural labourers, servants of landlords, tenants and members of depressed classes. With the amendment in Provincial Insolvency Act, the scope of the Act was broadened and now all those whose debts were Rs. 250 or above and value of whose property does not exceed Rs. 2,000 can go to the Insolvency court and could get himself declared an insolvent. Earlier only those persons could take advantage of

insolvency whose debts amounted to not less than Rs. 500 and whose property was not likely to exceed Rs. 5,000 in value.

(8) Two snags were observed in the working of this Act which thwarted the spirit of the Act namely, (a) Even if one of the joint creditors did not attend the hearing fixed, the Conciliation Board could not deliver the judgment and, (b) Unless the creditors whom the debtor owed 40 per cent of the debt agreed to submit their cases to the Conciliation Board and accept its award, the board remained a helpless spectator. These snags were removed from the Act by the 1940's amendment. Now this Act had the following main features:

(i) If the creditor or any of the joint creditors failed to be present in person or through his accredited agent at any of the hearings fixed by the Conciliation Board, or failed to produce full particulars and documents required under the Act, the debt payable to him or the joint creditors, whatever the case, was deemed as fully discharged for all purposes.

(ii) If the creditors refused to accept a seasonable offer made by the debtor, the Conciliation Board could issue a certificate in respect of such debts, which deprived such creditors of any interest (earlier it was allowed at 6% per annum) on the debts after the date of certification, and even if such a creditor succeeded in obtaining a decree from the court its execution was deferred till the claims of all those creditors, who had accepted the offer had been satisfied.

(iii) The rate of interest was lowered from 18¾ to 12½ per cent simple interest in case of unsecured loans and on secured debts it was lowered from 12 to 7½ per cent simple interest per annum and the compound interest was altogether abolished.

(iv) The principle of damdupat, which only applied to debt raised after 1934, under the original Act, henceforth covered all debts whether incurred before or after 1934.

(v) The Act also applied to all non-agriculturist debtors whether living in rural areas or urban areas, whose total net assets did not exceed Rs. 5,000 in value, to the extent that their one main residential house could not be attached or sold in the execution of a debt decree.

The amendments were also made in 1938 and 1939 in the Punjab Debtors Protection Act of 1936. The main features of this Act were:[59]

1. The period of the limitation of the execution of a debt decree was reduced from 12 to 6 years.
2. Civil courts could not lease out the land of the agriculturist debtor in satisfaction of a decree. Whenever the civil court orders that land be attached and alienated temporarily in the execution of a decree for the payment of the money the proceedings of such attachment and alienation were transferred to the collector.
3. The collector had to decide the period of alienation, which could not exceed twenty years in the case of land owned by the member of a statutory agricultural tribe.
4. Ancestral land and property was exempted from liability in the execution of a decree or order of a

59. The Punjab Debtors Protection Act, 1936 (Punjab Act No. II of 1936), *The Punjab Code,* Vol. II, Lahore, 1937, pp. 789-795 also *The Punjab Government Gazette, Extraordinary,* March 26, 1938 and also January 12, 1939, p. 1.

court relating to the debt incurred by any of his predecessor in interest.

5. Standing crops other than cotton and sugarcane and standing trees, ancestral property, furniture and some part of the land of the debtor were exempted from attachment.

Amendments were also made in the Punjab Agricultural Produce Markets Act in 1941 and 1944. To establish standards of measures and to regulate the use of weights and measures the Unionist Ministry also passed the Punjab Weights and Measures Act, 1941.[60] An amendment was also made in the Punjab Sugarcane Act of 1934 in 1943 to stop the malpractices of the factory staff such as false weighment, arbitrary objection to quality of cane, etc.[61]

In this way, a series of agrarian legislation was passed by the Punjab provincial government to help the peasants. These Acts and amendments gave some relief to the suffering peasantry who had many grievances such as indebtedness, transfer of their land to the moneylenders and their exploitation in the markets.

---

60. The Punjab Weights and Measures Act, 1941, *The Punjab Code*, Vol. II, 7th edition, Simla, 1953, pp. 965-985.
61. *The Punjab Sugarcane Act, 1934* (Indian Act No. XV of 1934) (As amended by Punjab Act IX of 1943), Lahore, 1944.

Summing Up

The peasant society in Haryana was divided into castes, tribes and classes. Each caste had its own occupation. Each tribe had their own customs, rituals and practices. During the late 19th century and early 20th century the caste system was not rigid but it became rigid when the British recorded the castes and tribes of the peasantry in the census, settlement reports, district gazetteers and other official records.

There were many problems which were created by the British rule such as agricultural backwardness, the imposition of high land revenue rates, indebtedness of the peasants and transfer of their land to the moneylenders. In the Haryana region, agriculture had developed much less due to lack of rainfall and artificial means of irrigation.

Therefore, in Haryana the peasants had to grow the crops which needed less water. The peasants grew food-cum-fodder crops because there was a great demand for food and fodder for the animals. The profession of agriculture was not profitable and the economic condition of the peasants remained precarious.

The British system of land revenue had also many problems. The assessment of land revenue was based only on the value of produce and ignored the cost of cultivation. The peasants thus had to pay a large proportion of their produce as land revenue. The British collected land revenue in cash only. Therefore the peasants had to take loans from moneylenders to pay the land revenue and other expenses.

In Haryana mostly peasants were small proprietors whose petty income often fell short of consumption needs. Therefore they had to borrow for subsistence. Here the big peasants were also in debt because the land revenue was levied on the land at a flat rate per acre and therefore large land owners or big peasants had to pay a large amount as a tax which even they could not afford to pay.

The other changes in the agrarian economy like recording of proprietary rights, introduction of tenancy legislation, commercialization of agriculture, steady rise in land value and the growing competition for acquisition of land complicated the agrarian scene. Owing to poor economic conditions in Haryana the relation between moneylenders and peasants, peasant proprietors and the tenants, peasants and agricultural labourers were strained. Other reasons like communalism, propaganda and rivalry were also responsible for this situation.

The process of politicization of the peasantry in the Haryana region started in the 1920s. By the Government of India Act 1919 the electorates were divided into urban and rural areas. By this act only candidates from 'agriculturist tribes' were allowed to fight the elections for the rural constituencies. Earlier the Government of India Act 1909 had divided the electorates on communal lines.

Due to the nationalist movement, the feelings of nationalism increased among the urban people. And this movement also started to win over the agriculturist class of the province but the colonial rulers wanted to keep them away from the influence of the nationalist movement. Therefore in the Punjab a further division in the electorates on rural and urban basis was introduced within the communal division.

Owing to the urban-rural division of electorates, a party, first called the Rural Bloc, then Rural Party, and later the Punjab National Unionist Party emerged in 1923. The era of peasant politics was started. By 'pro-agriculturist ideology and rural-oriented programmes', it dominated the politics of Haryana and the whole of Punjab for more than two decades.

During this period, the Congress Party concentrated on the freedom movement, which impacted Haryana as it did other parts of the country. It played an important role to mobilize the people against the colonial rule.

In the elections of 1937, when provincial autonomy was given, the Unionist Party emerged as the single largest powerful party in the Punjab and won a majority of seats. The success of the Unionist Party was the result of projecting their agrarian programmes as aimed at relieving the rural grievances. By these policies the Unionist Party was successful in the rural constituencies. In these elections the Congress Party had failed in gaining the support of the peasantry.

In the elections of 1946 the position of the Unionist Party declined. It had become unpopular among the peasants due to war time economic dislocations. The argument about the economic achievements of the party and call for inter-communal cooperation did not get a response from the peasantry. In these elections polarization of communities took place because of communalism. In the Haryana region Congress fared well, while in West Punjab the Muslim League won the majority of seats in these elections.

The Unionist Party enacted a series of legislations with the objective of improving the conditions of the agriculturist class in Haryana and the whole of Punjab. The government introduced many new Acts and amendments to existing Acts to give relief to the indebted peasants of the Punjab. These Acts were called "Golden Laws" by the supporters and opposition called them "Black Laws". These Acts were created for the redressal of the rural grievances and to help the agriculturist class. They gave relief to the indebted peasants and neutralized the malpractices of the moneylenders. These laws empowered the peasantry.

By these legislations the Unionist Party succeeded in getting support from the agriculturist class. The Unionist Party successfully mobilized the peasants in the rallies organized by its leaders in Haryana and other parts of the Punjab. The popularity of the party increased.

The Congress Party in Haryana played an important role in the freedom struggle. It reached out to the rural people to mobilize them against the colonial rule. It started the Non-Cooperation Movement, Civil Disobedience Movement and the Quit India Movement. It developed the anti-imperialist ideology among the peasants.

During the Non-Cooperation Movement, in August 1920, after the adoption of the non-cooperation resolution, many prominent leaders including Gandhiji, Muhammad Ali, Shaukat Ali, Abul Kalam Azad, Dr. M.A.Ansari, Neki Ram Sharma and Swami Satyadeva visited this region and addressed many meetings. These meetings promoted the programmes of mass enrolment of Congress workers, the collection of funds and the distribution of spinning-wheels. The anti-liquor and anti-foreign cloth campaign was also successful in Haryana.

As a part of boycott the British courts, many leading lawyers of the country gave up their lucrative practices. In Haryana panchayats began to dispose of petty cases without resorting to the courts. The litigants also boycotted the government courts and cases were taken to national courts. As a part of boycott of the educational institutes, thousands of students left schools and colleges and joined national schools and colleges that had sprung up all over the country. In the Haryana region the students responded the same way. Many schools and colleges disaffiliated themselves from Punjab University. Police used repressive measures to stop demonstrations and processions. After the incident of Chauri Chaura in Gorakhpur district of UP, Gandhiji withdrew the movement.

The Congress launched the Civil Disobedience Movement in 1930. Gandhiji started the movement from Dandi by picking up a handful of salt. Soon, all over the country, the defiance of salt law started. In the Haryana region people participated in this movement with great enthusiasm. The salt law was broken by preparing contraband salt. There were also many instances of picketing of liquor shops and boycott of foreign goods. As a result, the consumption of liquor decreased and the wholesale and retail business of cloth declined.

The Congress agitation was more active and successful in rural areas. In many districts Congress set up a parallel government by appointing officials. At many places the peasants refused to pay land revenue and taxes. In 1934, Gandhiji withdrew this movement.

The Individual Satyagraha was launched in 1940. In Haryana, many Congress leaders toured the villages and addressed public meetings. They were arrested for participation in civil disobedience. This movement continued for fifteen months when it was suspended by Gandhiji. The people of this region showed great passion for the movement.

Gandhiji also began the Quit India Movement on August 8, 1942. The next day the government arrested all the top leaders of the Congress Party. They were taken to unknown destinations. All over the country people expressed their anger by attacking police stations, post offices, courts, railway stations and other symbols of government authority. National flags were hoisted on public buildings in many places. The Congress Party was declared an unlawful organization and its offices were locked. The government crushed the movement by using harsh measures.

Another movement, the pro-Indian National Army (INA) Movement emerged in mid-1945. A nation-wide agitation was started against the British policy of punishing the three main INA officers—Maj. Gen. Shah Nawaz Khan,

Lt. Col. P.K. Sehgal and Lt. Col. G.S. Dhillon. The people in general, students, political parties and even armed forces showed their sympathy towards INA officials and personnel. Many parts of Haryana observed complete 'hartal' and several meetings were held. The INA anti-recruitment propaganda took place in some districts of Haryana and also occurred in the Delhi recruiting area.

The Indian National Congress demanded the unconditional release of INA personnel. The Punjab Provincial Congress Committee prepared a memorandum for submission to the Viceroy and the Commander-in-Chief. The British realized the situation and Commander-in-Chief remitted the sentence of transportation passed by the court martial against the INA officers and they were set free.

During these movements many nationalist leaders with the local leaders visited this region and addressed many meetings. The people of Haryana participated with great enthusiasm in these movements. The nationalist movement was successful in mobilizing the peasants against the imperial rule.

The Indian National Movement led by the Indian National Congress was also successful in spreading the feeling of nationalism among the peasantry. The peasants were aware of the colonial exploitation and participated in the national movement due to which it became a mass movement and was victorious in overthrowing the colonial rule.

Bibliography

(a) Primary Sources

National Archives of India (NAI), New Delhi.
Records of Home Political Department.
Punjab Fortnightly Reports and Other States, 1920-46.
Government of India, Home Political (Internal) Files.
Intelligence Bureau Record (Home Departments) Files.

Haryana State Archives (HSA), Panchkula
District Records

Deputy Commissioner Offices Records – Ambala and Rohtak District.
Superintendent of Police Offices Records – Rohtak District.

Papers

All India Congress Committee Papers, 1921-45, NMML, New Delhi.
Gopi Chand Bhargava Papers, 1937-45, NMML, New Delhi.
Linlithgow Papers, 1936-43, NMML, New Delhi.
Neki Ram Sharma Papers, 1908-53, NMML, New Delhi.
Sardar Sunder Singh Majithia Papers, 1921-42, NMML, New Delhi.

Official Publications

(i) Settlement Reports
Settlement Report of the Karnal District, 1883.
Settlement Report of the Karnal District, 1909.
Settlement Report of the Rohtak District, 1880.
Settlement Report of the Rohtak District, 1910.

(ii) District Gazetteers

Hissar, 1892.
Karnal, 1910.
Rohtak, 1918.

(iii) Board of Economic Inquiry, Punjab (BEIP)

Village Surveys of
Bhadas, Gurgaon District, 1936.
Gijhi, Rohtak District, 1932.
Naggal, Ambala District, 1933.

(iv) Indian Statutory Commission, Volume XVI, Selection from Memoranda and Oral Evidence by Non-Officials (Part 1), London 1930.

(v) Other Official Reports

Census of India, Punjab, 1881, 1891, 1901, 1911, 1921, 1931.
J.M. Douie, Punjab Settlement Manual, First Published in 1899 and Reprint 1985, Lahore.
Punjab Legislative Assembly Debates, 1937-46, Lahore.
Punjab Legislative Council Debates, 1921-35, Lahore.
Report of the Land Revenue Committee, Punjab, Lahore, 1938.
Report of the Punjab Provincial Banking Enquiry Committee, 1929-30, Vol. 1, Lahore, 1930.

(vi) Other Official Publications

Indian Annual Register (1919-47), N.N. Mitra, New Delhi, 1990.
The Punjab Code, Vol. I, Lahore, 1937.
The Punjab Code, Vol. II, Lahore, 1937.
The Punjab Code, Vol. II, Simla, 1953.
Transfer of Power Papers (1942-47), Vol. VI-VII, New Delhi, 1976.

Unofficial Publications

Bingley, A.H., *Caste Handbooks for the Indian Army: Brahmans*, Simla, 1897.

________, *Handbook for the Indian Army: Jats, Gujars and Ahirs*, New Delhi, 1941.

Calvert, H., *The Wealth and Welfare of the Punjab*, Lahore, 1936.

Darling, M.L., *The Punjab Peasant in Prosperity and Debt*, Columbia, 1925.

________, *Rusticus Loquitor, or the Old Light and the New in the Punjab Villages*, London, 1930.

________, *Wisdom and Waste in the Punjab Village*, London, 1934, Reprint, Delhi, 1977.

Macmunn, G.F., *Armies of India*, London, 1911.

Stowe, A.M., *Cattle and Dairying in the Punjab*, Lahore, 1910.

Trevaskis, H.K., *An Economic History of Punjab (1890-1925)*, Vol. II, Lahore 1931.

Other Unofficial Publications

Carter, Lionel, ed., *Punjab Politics*, 1936-1939: The Start of Provincial Autonomy – Governors' Fortnightly Reports and Other Key Documents, New Delhi: Manohar Publishers, 2004.

Chatterji, Basudev, ed., *Towards Freedom: Documents on the Movement for Independence in India*, 1938, Part-3, New Delhi: Oxford University Press, 1999.

Newspapers

Civil and Military Gazette, Lahore
Hindustan Times, New Delhi
The Tribune, Lahore.

(b) Secondary Sources

Books and Articles

Baden-Powell, B.H., *The Land System of British India*, Reprint, London: Oriental Publishers, 1972.

Banerjee, Himadri, *Agrarian Society of the Punjab (1849-1901)*, New Delhi: Manohar Publications, 1982.

________, 'Changes in Agrarian Society in the Late Nineteenth Century' in *Five Punjabi Centuries: Polity, Economy, Society and Culture, C. 1500-1900*, ed. by Indu Banga, New Delhi: Manohar Publishers, 1997.

Barrier, Norman G., 'The Formulation and Enactment of the Punjab Alienation of Land Bill', in the *Punjab Past and Present*, Vol. XIII-I, April 1979, S. No. 25, Punjabi University, Patiala.

Bayly, C.A., *Rulers., Townsmen and Bazaars: North Indian Society in the Age of British Expansion, 1770-1870*, Delhi: OUP, 1992.

________, *Empire and Information: Intelligence Gathering and Social Communication in India, 1780-1870*, Cambridge: CUP, 1996.

Bayly, Susan, *Caste, Society and Politics in India From the Eighteenth Century to the Modern Age*, CUP, Cambridge, 1999.

Bhattacharya, Neeladri, 'Lenders and Debtors: Punjab Countryside, 1880-1940', in *Studies in History*, 1, 2, New Series (1985).

Caton, Brian P., 'Social Categories and Colonialisation in Punjab, 1849-1920', *The Indian Economic and Social History Review*, 41, 1 (2004).

Chander, Jagdish, 'Political Development in Haryana 1928-47' in *Haryana: Studies in History and Politics*, ed. by J.N. Singh Yadav, New Delhi: Manohar Publications, 1976.

Chandra, Bipan, *The Rise and Growth of Economic Nationalism in India*, New Delhi: People's Publishing House, 1966.

Chandra, Bipan, et al., *India's Struggle for Independence*, New Delhi: Penguin Books, 1989.

Chandra, Bipan, *Modern India*, New Delhi: National Council of Educational Research and Training (NCERT), 1990.

Chatterjee, Partha, 'Agrarian Relations and Communalism in Bengal 1926-35', *Subaltern Studies 1, Writings on South Asian History and Society*, ed. by Ranajit Guha, Delhi: Oxford University Press, 1982.

Chowdhry, Prem, Rural Relations Prevailing in the Punjab at the Time of the Enactment of the So-Called 'Golden Laws' or Agrarian Legislations of the Late Thirties, in the *Punjab Past and Present*, Vol. X-II, October 1976.

________, 'The Congress Triumph in South-East Punjab: Elections of 1946', *Studies in History*, Vol. II, No. 2 (1980).

________, *Punjab Politics: The Role of Sir Chhotu Ram*, New Delhi: Vikas Publishing House, 1984.

________, 'The Advantages of Backwardness: Colonial Policy and Agriculture in Haryana', in *The Economic and Social History Review*, 23, 3 (1986), New Delhi.

Cohn, Bernard S., 'The Census, Social Structure and Objectification in South Asia' in Cohn, *An Anthropologist Among the Historians and Other Essays*, Delhi: Oxford University Press, 1987.

________, *Colonialism and Its Forms of Knowledge: The British in India*, Delhi: Oxford University Press, 1997.

Crooke, W., *Races of Northern India*, Delhi: Cosmo Publications, 1973.

Desai, A.R. (ed.), *Peasant Struggles in India*, Delhi: Oxford University Press, 1979.

Dirks, Nicholas B., *Caste of Mind: Colonialism and the Making of Modern India*, Princeton: Princeton University Press, 2001.

Dutt, R.C., *The Economic History of India* (2 Vols.), London, 1902, Reprint, Delhi: Low Price Publications, 1990, 1995.

Dutt, R.P., *India Today*, Bombay: People's Publishing House, 1947.

Ghosh, K.K., *Indian National Army*, Meerut: Meenakshi Prakashan, 1969.

Gilmartin, David, 'Religious Leadership and the Pakistan Movement in the Punjab', *Modern Asian Studies*, 13, 3 (1979).

________, *Empire and Islam: Punjab and the Making of Pakistan*, Delhi: Oxford University Press, 1989.

Gopal, Madan, *Sir Chhotu Ram: A Political Biography*, Delhi: B.R. Publishing, 1977.

________, *Sir Chhotu Ram: The Man and The Vision*, Ghaziabad: Bhagirath Seva Sansthan Publication Division, 1997.

Guha, Ranajit, *Elementary Aspects of Peasant Insurgency in Colonial India*,

Delhi: Oxford University Press, 1983.

Hardiman, David, (ed.), *Peasant Resistance in India, 1858-1914*, Delhi: Oxford University Press, 1992.

Ibbetson, Denzil, *Panjab Castes*, 1916, Reprint, Delhi: Cosmo Publications, 1974.

Mahajan, Sucheta, *Independence and Partition*, New Delhi: Sage Publications, 2000.

Malik, Ikram Ali, *The History of Punjab, 1799-1947*, New Delhi: Neeraj Publications, 1970.

Metcalf, Thomas R., *Ideologies of the Raj*, New Delhi: Cambridge University Press, 1995.

Mukherjee, Mridula, 'Some Aspects of Agrarian Structure of Punjab, 1925-47', in *Economic and Political Weekly*, Vol. XV, No. 26, June, 1980.

________, Peasant Resistance and Peasant Consciousness in Colonial India (Subaltern and Beyond), *Economic and Political Weekly*, October, 1988.

________, *Peasants in India's Non Violent Revolution: Practice and Theory*, New Delhi: Sage Publications, 2004.

________, *Colonializing Agriculture: The Myth of Punjab Exceptionalism*, New Delhi: Sage Publications, 2005.

Pandey, Deepak, 'The Social Base of Unionist Party', *Punjab History Conference*, 13th Session, March, 1979.

Pandey, Gyan, 'Peasant Revolt and Indian Nationalism: The Peasant Movement in Awadh 1919-22', *Selected Subaltern Studies* ed. by Ranajit Guha and Gayatri Chakravorty Spivak, Delhi: Oxford University Press, 1988.

Rai, Satya M., *Legislative Politics and the Freedom Struggle in the Punjab, 1897-1947*, New Delhi: Indian Council of Historical Research, 1984.

Randhawa, M.S., *A History of Agriculture in India*, Vol. III, *1757-1947*, New Delhi: Indian Council of Agricultural Research, 1983.

Ranga, N.G., *Revolutionary Peasants*, New Delhi: Amrit Book Co., 1949.

Rathee, Anil Kumar and Nandal, D.S., *Sir Chhotu Ram and Punjab Economy Under Imperialism*, Rohtak: Spellbound Publications, 1997.

Risley, H.H., *The People of India*, Calcutta: Thacker, Spink & Co., 1915.

Rose, H.A., *A Glossary of the Tribes and Castes of the Punjab and Northwest Frontier Province*, First Published in 1919, Reprint, Delhi: Amar Prakashan, 1980.

Said, Edward W., *Orientalism*, New Delhi: Penguin Books, 2001.

Sen, Sunil, *Peasants Movement in India: Mid Ninteenth and Twentieth*

Centuries, Calcutta: K.P. Bagchi, 1982.

Sharma, Inderjit, *Land Revenue Administration in the Punjab (1849-1901)*, New Delhi: Atlantic Publishers, 1985.

Singh, Amarjit, *Punjab Divided: Politics of Muslim League and Partition, 1935-45*, New Delhi: Kanishka Publications, 2001.

Singh, Anita Inder, *The Origin of the Partition of India*, Delhi: Oxford University Press, 1987.

Singh, Pardaman, *Chhotu Ram in the Eyes of His Contemporaries*, New Delhi: Gitanjali Publishing House, 1992.

Stokes, Eric, *The Peasant and the Raj: Studies in Agrarian Society and Peasant Rebellion in Colonial India*, Delhi: Vikas Publishing House, 1978.

Talbot, I.A., 'The 1946 Punjab Election', *Modern Asian Studies*, 14, 1 (1980).

________, 'Deserted Collaborators: The Political Background to the Rise and Fall of the Punjab Unionist Party, 1923-1947', in the *Journal of Imperial and Commonwealth History*, Vol. XI, October 1982.

________, *Punjab and the Raj (1849-1947)*, New Delhi: Manohar Publishers, 1988.

Verma, D.C., *Haryana*, New Delhi: National Book Trust, 1990.

Tanwar, Raghuvendra, *Politics of Sharing Power: The Punjab Unionist Party, 1923-47*, New Delhi: Manohar Publishers, 1999.

Wagnor, Phillip B., 'Precolonial Intellectuals and the Production of Colonial Knowledge', in *Comparative Studies in Society and History*, Vol. 45, No. 4, October 2003.

Wallace, Paul, 'Peasant Mobilization in India and the Contemporary Political Significance of Sir Chhotu Ram', in *Indian Journal of Political Science*, Vol. 41, No. 1, March 1980.

Yadav, K.C., *Elections in Punjab, 1920-47*, Delhi: Manohar Publications, 1987.

________, 'The Struggle for Freedom: Haryana, 1885-1947', *Journal of Haryana Studies*, Vol. XVII-XVIII, 1995-96, Kurukshetra: Kurukshetra University, Haryana.

________ (ed.), *The Crisis in India: Reflections of Sir Chhotu Ram*, Kurukshetra: Haryana Historical Society, 1996.

________, *Modern Haryana: History and Culture, 1803-1966*, New Delhi: Manohar Publications, 2002.

Yong, Tan Tai, *The Garrison State: The Military, Government and Society in Colonial Punjab, 1849-1947*, New Delhi: Sage Publications, 2005.

Index